Joseph Itiel

Sex Workers As Virtual Boyfriends

D1248285

More pre-publication
REVIEWS, COMMENTARIES, EVALUATIONS . . .

"In *Sex Workers As Virtual Boyfriends,*
Joseph Itiel has served up from his
many years of experience a smorgas-
board of brief and long-term encounters that will delight the reader. This
book is the perfect follow-up to his successful and entertaining *A Consumer's
Guide to Male Hustlers.* The basic princi-
ples for both sex workers and their clients that he outlined there are illus-
trated in detail here, giving both sides a
clearer understanding of what makes
paid sexual contacts work. Best of all,
he does it in his own unique narrative
style, full of wit and charm. There are
intriguing anecdotes of happy sexual
adventures from Toronto to Barcelona,
but the focus of his activity is San Francisco, whose variety of ethnic possibili-
ties has seldom been so widely ex-
plored. The reader will gain insights for
his own use—and in the most entertaining way. A fun read!"

Hubert Kennedy, PhD
Research Associate,
Center for Research and Education
in Sexuality,
San Francisco State University,
California

Harrington Park Press®
An Imprint of The Haworth Press, Inc.
New York • London • Oxford

Sex Workers
As Virtual Boyfriends

HARRINGTON PARK PRESS
New, Recent, and Forthcoming
Titles of Related Interest

Gay and Gray: The Older Homosexual Man, Second Edition by Raymond M. Berger

Against My Better Judgment: An Intimate Memoir of an Eminent Gay Psychologist by Roger Brown

The Masculine Marine: Homoeroticism in the U.S. Marine Corps by Steven Zeeland

Autopornography: A Memoir of Life in the Lust Lane by Scott "Spunk" O'Hara

The Empress Is a Man: Stories from the Life of José Sarria by Michael R. Gorman

A Consumer's Guide to Male Hustlers by Joseph Itiel

It's a Queer World: Deviant Adventures in Pop Culture by Mark Simpson

Macho Love: Sex Behind Bars in Central America by Jacobo Schifter

When It's Time to Leave Your Lover: A Guide for Gay Men by Neil Kaminsky

Tricks and Treats: Sex Workers Write About Their Clients edited by Matt Bernstein Sycamore

Gay Men at Midlife: Age Before Beauty by Alan L. Ellis

Finding a Lover for Life: A Gay Man's Guide to Finding Mr. Right by David Price

The Man Who Was a Woman and Other Queer Tales from Hindu Lore by Devdutt Pattanaik

Barrack Buddies and Soldier Lovers: Dialogues with Gay Young Men in the U.S. Military by Steven Zeeland

Rebel Yell: Stories by Contemporary Southern Gay Authors edited by Jay Quinn

Sissyphobia: Gay Men and Effeminate Behavior by Tim Bergling

Sex Terror: Erotic Misadventures in Pop Culture by Mark Simpson

Sex Workers As Virtual Boyfriends by Joseph Itiel

Tops, Bottom, and Versatiles: The Meanings of Anal Sex for Gay Men by Steven G. Underwood

Escapades of a Gay Traveler: Sexual, Cultural, and Spiritual Encounters by Joseph Itiel

Sex Workers
As Virtual Boyfriends

Joseph Itiel

Harrington Park Press®
An Imprint of The Haworth Press, Inc.
New York • London • Oxford

Published by

Harrington Park Press®, an imprint of The Haworth Press, Inc., 10 Alice Street, Binghamton, NY 13904-1580.

PUBLISHER'S NOTE
In all case studies, names, selected data, and corporate identities have been disguised.

Cover design by Anastasia Litwak.

Library of Congress Cataloging-in-Publication Data

Itiel, Joseph.
    Sex workers as virtual boyfriends / Joseph Itiel.
       p. cm.
    A companion volume to the author's A consumer's guide to male hustlers.
    "Sex workers' web sites": p.
    ISBN 1-56023-190-4 (alk. paper : hard) — ISBN 1-56023-191-2 (alk. paper : soft)
    1. Male prostitution. 2. Male friendship. 3. Sex instruction for gay men. 4. Gay men—Sexual behavior. I. Itiel, Joseph. Consumer's guide to male hustlers. II. Title.

HQ76.1 .I88 2002
306.74'3—dc21

2001039560

Also by Joseph Itiel

Financial Well-Being Through Self-Hypnosis

The Franz Document

Philippine Diary: A Gay Guide to the Philippines

De Onda: A Gay Guide to Mexico and Its People

Pura Vida: A Gay and Lesbian Guide to Costa Rica

A Consumer's Guide to Male Hustlers

ABOUT THE AUTHOR

Joseph Itiel likes to say that in his senior years he has been blessed with great (and affordable) sex workers. But this is not just a lucky coincidence. The author met his first hustlers—as they were called then—some forty years ago. He has had the time and perseverance to shape these commercial encounters into virtual friendships. Itiel makes his home in San Francisco, California.

CONTENTS

Preface   ix

Acknowledgments   xiii

Prologue. Would *I* Make a Good Sex Worker?   1

Chapter 1. Do Sex Workers Hustle and Are Their Johns
Clients?   11

Chapter 2. Agencies, the Internet, and Advance Bookings   21

Chapter 3. Tarred by the Straight Brush   31

Chapter 4. The New Professionalism—Does It Benefit
Clients?   41

Chapter 5. Ass to Ass: The Tantra Massage   47

Chapter 6. Sex-Plus Relationships   55

Chapter 7. Playing Prisoner of War   65

Chapter 8. "I Used to Be Joseph's Little Prostitute"   73

Chapter 9. Defaulting to Sex Work   85

Chapter 10. Sugar Daddies and Their Ungrateful Sons   97

Chapter 11. Sex Work for Better Self-Esteem   109

Chapter 12. "Mature" Sex Workers   117

Chapter 13. Seven Guidelines   125

Appendix: Sex Workers' Web Sites   137

Notes   139

Index   143

Preface

Not long ago, Michael, my regular sex worker, had a fistfight and wound up with a fat lip. In the three-and-a-half years we have known each other, he has never been involved in a physical confrontation. "What happened?" I asked him.

"This guy I've been dating—not escorting—had too much to drink. He wanted us to become boyfriends. I told him that I wasn't looking for no boyfriend. That's when he punched me." Michael was quite upset by the incident and kept talking about it. When we got into bed I gave him a kiss and said, "Well, Michael, at least we have each other."

"That's true," he answered.

Both of us understood perfectly well what I meant by "having each other." We do have each other for our sessions but certainly not "for better or for worse." However much we like and enjoy each other, Michael will see me only if, at the end of each session, I hand him his fee. I will use his services only as long as I don't get the same for free from someone else. Because, you see, we are only *virtual* boyfriends. Nonetheless, this virtual relationship, not to be confused with the *real* thing, has worked exceedingly well for both of us.

The overall purpose of this book is to help readers "upgrade" their sex workers (formerly known as hustlers) into *virtual* boyfriends. Not all sex workers can be or wish to be upgraded; nor do all clients want their sex workers to become their virtual boyfriends. But some men who engage sex workers on a regular basis might prefer to experience deeper relationships with them. This book offers real-life experiences and practical ways to accomplish such a transition.

This book is also a continuation and amplification of my previous work, *A Consumer's Guide to Male Hustlers*.[1] It can be understood fully without reading the former book. However, *A Consumer's Guide to Male Hustlers* is a primer for this book. I will not repeat here the information contained in the former work. For instance, I will take for granted that readers are familiar with the health and safety issues I have discussed at length in my original book, and the distinction I have made between male and female prostitution. I recommend to readers who feel that they have benefited from this work to acquaint themselves with the previous publication.

Although meaningful sex worker/client interaction cannot be taught, it can be described. To this end, I will sketch a number of my sex workers, past and present, dead and alive, and tell our stories. In these sketches, I try to bring out the marvelous uniqueness of each sex worker. Through this uniqueness, clients can match their requirements and resources to sex workers who will fulfill their needs. Clients who have the most satisfaction are invariably the ones who are attuned to how *different* individual sex workers are.

Finding the right sex worker and becoming virtual boyfriends sometimes takes considerable effort. In this book I describe my search for a second regular sex worker —Michael's understudy. This account will serve readers well in their own quest.

This book is written for gay men with some financial means at their disposal. Neither the fabulously wealthy nor those in financially difficult circumstances may be able to sustain the type of sex worker relationship I describe. The first, because such a relationship is prone to degenerate into "sugar daddyism"; the latter, because they do not have the wherewithal to see sex workers on a regular basis.

In my previous book I began with the premise that hustlers are independent contractors. As such, they are an equal party in negotiating and conducting the sex session. Continuing with this premise, this book also assumes that sex workers are completely independent agents. *This definition automatically excludes sex workers employed by male brothels or agencies, as well as minors who are not competent to negotiate as equal partners.*

My current sex worker and I are not in love with each other and, naturally, I pay for his services. But we genuinely care about each other. Physically, the attraction is one sided. Michael is my type; I am not his. But both of us are comfortable physically and emotionally with each other. The fondness I feel for Michael I have not been able to achieve with most of my cruising pickups over a period of some forty years. Flying in the face of conventional gay wisdom, I have witnessed that, by and large, my contacts with sex workers have been physically and psychologically more fulfilling, safer, and often more elegant than those with my cruising pickups. In sharing these experiences with readers, I hope to shed more light on successful interaction with sex workers for the benefit of *both* parties.

Acknowledgments

A number of friends have helped me with this book. I wish to acknowledge them and express my deep gratitude. David Klein, all the way from San Ramón de Alajuela in Costa Rica, has edited the manuscript. As always, my friend Howard Curtis has contributed his insights. Bob Kane has put at my disposal his private library. Hubert Kennedy has given me stylistic guidance. Kirk Read has made valuable suggestions. Escort "R" has encouraged me to see things from the sex worker's point of view. Last but not least, my regular sex worker Michael has expedited the writing of the manuscript by allowing me to focus on the work at hand rather than waste time chasing after elusive, free-access partners.

AUTHOR'S NOTE

All characters in this book are real. However, I have taken great pains to change not only their names but also their physical and ethnic descriptions, as well as their places of origin and the work they do. Consequently, any similarity to living or dead persons is purely coincidental.

Prologue

Would *I* Make a Good Sex Worker?

Sex workers have told me a great deal about themselves. But hearing stories is not the same as experiencing them. If I were *a lot* younger and wanted to write about male prostitution, I would try out "sex working" to get the feel of it. But at my age, this option is not open to me.

If I cannot be a real sex worker, it would behoove me to experience, even if only once, all aspects of the issues I write about. In Chapter 8 of *A Consumer's Guide to Male Hustlers,* I described how I pretended that I was a hustler to find out whether it was possible to psych oneself into this role. Surprisingly, I discovered that the psyching was a piece of cake.

In my experiment, I managed to psych myself into an assumed hustler role. But I had to do a lot of it to play the role credibly. Ordinarily, my personal taste in men is focused very narrowly on specific physical types of a limited age range.

The moment of truth came when my make-believe client asked me to screw him. I was afraid that my dick would betray me. He was the antithesis of my favorite physical type and forty years out of my ideal age range. Until that moment, the psyching had been passive and therefore easy to accomplish. But how would I perform when called upon to prove *actively,* through an unflagging erection, a sexual desire for this man? Fortunately, the client backed down. He said that he was too old for this sort of thing. I would have tried to accommodate him, but I suspect that performance anxiety alone might have undermined my good intentions.

Afterward, I discussed this particular subject with many sex workers. The ones who top their clients routinely often attribute their hard dicks and ability to penetrate upon demand to their youthful sexual vigor. But I know older sex workers who are equally competent. After many interviews, I came to believe that they arouse themselves through the excitement of their partners. Just seeing and feeling their clients' arousal helps them become hard, maintain their erections, and perform their duty. One could say that they do it with mirrors. Would I also be able to experience arousal as an echo of my partner's sexual stimulation?

In my particular circumstance, the experiment would be conducted in a "lab," as it were, where I would assume the role of a sex worker. (Yes, I too upgraded myself from hustler to sex worker!) The last time around, my lab was a Berkeley bathhouse. There I had created a situation in which I made myself available to the first man who wanted me and took care of his sexual needs *regardless* of my own preferences.

This time, I thought that the most effective way to start would be to advertise on an Internet personals board. In my ad, I would give a lot of information about myself. Based on this information, whoever answered my ad would be reasonably sure I was his type. As far as my partner went, all I would ask for was a "fun" bottom of any age and of any ethnic group. Such an ad would be broad enough to include the entire bottom cohort of the San Francisco Bay Area. The "fun" description had to be added just to make my ad credible. After all, I would have to mention *some* quality I desired in my partner. The vast majority of bottoms consider themselves "fun." In my ad, I would specify "safe only." Like me, professional sex workers would also be unwilling to "bareback" their clients.

In my experiment, the client would pay me, but only virtually. To simulate the sex-for-money exchange, I would schedule the event on a day I would normally see Michael, my regular sex worker. In other words, I would take care of my client *instead* of meeting Michael. If a penny saved is a penny earned, I would be "paid" $50 by my client— that is, the money I would not give Michael on that day.

Being a top is far from my favorite role. Before the client arrived, I would premedicate myself with 50 mg of Viagra. This would not distort the results of the experiment. A lot of top sex workers, however young, use Viagra (which they can buy on the Internet).[1]

Having worked out experiment protocol, I placed the ad on Yahoo's "Male to Male Personals" site. There must be a corollary to Murphy's Law that states, "When you want things to go wrong they will turn out perfectly right." The point of the experiment was to meet someone I did not care for physically and, in spite of it, manage to top him successfully. Just as in my Berkeley experiment, my first respondent, Roland, was a dream man. He was a thirty-five-year-old handsome Caucasian. Even though I usually prefer darker types, I liked Roland's soulful blue eyes and his boyish face. He was well educated, a world traveler, owned a house in San Francisco and a cottage at the Russian River, worked as a general manager of a Silicon Valley dot-com company, and probably held many stock options. He was hairy, usually a turnoff for me, but trimmed it neatly. Fortunately, he had no facial hair. Once at my place, he asked sheepishly whether it would be all right if we dispensed with the screwing part and just made love. This request made things even better. We were completely compatible.

Of course, the experiment had to be set aside because nothing useful could be learned from it. Maybe, I mused, my energy should go into making Roland my lover rather than researching male prostitution.

But when we were done, Roland said, "Well, thanks for a wonderful time. You know, I have a lover my own age."

Damn, I thought. Was *he* also conducting some weird experiment? "Why did you answer my ad, then?" I asked. "I'm almost twice your lover's age."

"I don't know why, but I like older men. Every now and then I have this urge to have sex with one. But, of course, I can't let this get out of hand. I'm happy with my lover. This will be *our* little secret."

"Will I ever see you again?"

"Not for a long while. Don't misunderstand me; I enjoyed myself. You're such a nice man. But I don't want this to become a habit."

* * *

The second serious respondent was a man named James. According to his own physical description, he was an ordinary forty-nine-year-old Caucasian gentleman who enjoyed being penetrated by an older top. He emphasized that discretion was a must. His emphasis on discretion amused me. Did he think that I would invite friends and relatives to view the performance?

We exchanged photographs. James replied that I was just what he had been fantasizing about. His picture showed only the front of his body from the neck down to his thighs. I wondered why he had not sent me a photo showing his face. Was it because of the discretion issue or because he was extremely ugly? Michael tells me that when he meets a new john he concentrates on one part of the man's body he likes. From the photo, I knew James's compact dick was passable. If his face was horrid, I would follow Michael's way of coping by focusing on James's dick.

I e-mailed James, gave him my phone number, and asked him to call me. I have made the acquaintance of a number of sex partners (free and for fee) on the Internet. I have always insisted that we speak on the phone before we make a date. I consider myself a good phone interviewer. I am reluctant to allow a stranger in my home (or to go to his place) without some form of prior verbal communication.

James turned out to be a prompt person. I had written him that he could reach me from eight o'clock in the evening onward. He called at 8:01. He had a pleasant, deep voice and appeared to be well educated. "My partner of many years turned eighty a few months ago. Unfortunately, he can't perform sexually any longer," James informed me. "He has been wonderful to me for all these years so I'm not complaining. But I'm looking. . . ."

"Look no more," I wanted to say, "you have been accepted into my experiment." Instead, I told him that I would like to meet him as soon as possible. "I'll take good care of you," I assured him.

"By the way," James asked, "do you like foreplay?"

"For instance?"

"Kissing, cuddling, that sort of thing."

This is what I am all about, I thought to myself. My problem with James would be that, for me, kissing has always been a more intimate activity than penetration either way. Over the years, I have found that this is not unusual. My sex workers are all great kissers; otherwise, they wouldn't be *my* workers. But I have run into quite a few who were willing to screw or get screwed but not French kiss. For them, too, it is a more intimate activity than penetration. Playing at being a versatile and accomplished sex worker, I told James, "Kissing would be OK."

We made a date for Thursday, three days in the future, at ten in the morning. He would call me on Thursday at eight to confirm. Deliberately, I didn't give him my address. This was another item on my agenda that I preferred to communicate in writing.

As the host, I would be called upon to observe some social amenities. I would ask my guest to sit in the living room for a few minutes while we exchanged pleasantries. Offering him a cup of coffee would be the polite thing to do. But such socializing could bring about two equally undesired consequences, either of which would interfere with my ability to go through with the experiment. If I disliked James thoroughly as a person and was not attracted to him physically, it would make it all the more difficult for me to make love to him. If I liked him as a person but felt physically repulsed by him, I would feel like a hypocrite while kissing, cuddling, and screwing him. Without the socializing, I would know nothing about him. It would be easier this way. Paradoxically, I myself insist on lots of "foretalk" from all my sex workers.

A day after our phone conversation, I e-mailed James my street address and added, "It would be an enormous turn-on for me if we plopped into bed immediately upon your arrival. We'll socialize when we're done."

On the morning of our planned date, at one minute past eight, James called to confirm. "You have my address?" I asked.

"Yes."

I knew then that he also had read my suggestion not to socialize before sex.

After James called, I turned on the computer and looked at his faceless photo once again. Yes, he had a decent dick. If I found I didn't like him, I would focus on his cock.

Half an hour before his scheduled arrival time, I took my 50 mg of Viagra. I prepared the condom and the lubricant. The clock struck ten and, simultaneously, the doorbell rang. I forced myself not to look through the peephole. If I was too grossed out by what I saw on the other side, I might be tempted not to let him in. I put on a happy face and opened the door widely, welcoming my client.

The person standing in front of me was a somewhat overweight Caucasian male of medium height, about sixty-five years old. His face was furrowed, and his head had only thin patches of hair scattered randomly. James was a plain-looking elderly gentleman, neither handsome nor ugly. Had I gone cruising, I would never have noticed him. His story about his eighty-year-old lover made more sense with only a fifteen-year age difference between them.

"Hi, James," I said in a friendly voice, extending my hand. As soon as he was inside the house, I ushered him wordlessly into my dedicated sex room. "Shall we get comfortable?" I asked.

I had no physical interest whatsoever in James. I was also somewhat resentful that he had lied about his age. Did he really think that he could pass for forty-nine? But as a sex worker I had no legitimate complaint against him. Workers are supposed to take on clients of all ages. We undressed in silence. At some point he remarked that it was an unseasonably cool day. I replied tersely, "Sure is." When we were both naked, I glanced at his dick. It was, indeed, a pleasant enough appendage. James hesitated momentarily, wondering what to do next. I guided him onto the bed and said, "Lie down and relax." He lay on his back and closed his eyes.

Of all unlikely thoughts, a quote from *Macbeth* popped into my head: "If it were done . . . then 'twere well it were done quickly." This is from Macbeth's soliloquy, just before readying himself to murder the sleeping King Duncan, a guest in his home, lying in bed much like James. "For heaven's sake," I reproached myself, "stop this melodrama." All *I* was called upon to do was kiss, cuddle, and screw James, nothing as repugnant as having to murder him.

I lay on top of him. Right away, I started French-kissing him in earnest. My unexpected aggressive kissing took James by surprise, and he moaned softly with pleasure. Underneath me, I could feel his cock springing to attention. As if we had choreographed our mating dance, my dick responded—not as much as his but, still, readying itself. We thrashed around for a while, and then I took his somewhat smallish cock into my mouth. James groaned with pleasure. For the next ten minutes we were making out. James was obviously turned on by me. I was on automatic pilot, just doing my job. As long as no interruptions occurred, everything would be fine.

Twice during this period, when James was on top of me and could see my face, he asked, "Are you all right?"

I had no idea why he asked me this. Had I faltered? Had I made an involuntary grimace? My answer both times was a terse, "I'm OK." Other than that, we were bent on pleasing each other.

I kept fretting in my mind about the inevitable upcoming interruption: the donning and lubrication of the condom. I hadn't performed this procedure in quite a while and was rusty. It might take me a full minute to do it right. I was afraid that this momentary distraction would make me lose my erection.

Much of the time I kept my eyes closed. I did not fantasize about other more appealing partners. Psyched up to perform my role as sex worker, my mind was focused on responding passionately to James's lovemaking and, periodically, taking the initiative myself. Most of all, I wanted to get the penetration chore out of the way. "I need to prepare myself to fuck you," I told James. I sat up. From the floor I retrieved the condom and the lube. James turned over and lay on his belly.

Now my eyes were wide open. I recalled from memory the various safe(r) sex instructions on how to put on and lubricate a condom. While doing this, I had a chance to survey my partner's ass. It probably had never been the best part of his body, and age was not kind to it. It was a fat, flabby, and shapeless ass, strewn with pimples and blemishes. Beholding this sorry sight, the detumescence of my erection was alarmingly fast. The proof was the shriveled condom.

In *A Consumer's Guide* (p. 94) I write about a hustler named Alfonso who always *pretended* to climax when he screwed his johns. (This was before AIDS. There were no telltale condoms to worry about.) It was Alfonso who had asked me rhetorically, "Who would want to screw a tired old ass?" My situation was much worse than Alfonso's. From his work, he had ample experience with all sorts of asses. I, on the other hand, had very little exposure in this area. Not being particularly fond of penetration, all the asses I have visited were of the sexy variety.

"Give me the lube," James said. I put the plastic vial in his left hand. Without changing his face-down position, he applied it liberally to his asshole.

Long ago, Michael had told me that if everything else failed, he focused on what he would do with the money the john gave him. My thought was that $50 was far too little for what I was being called upon to do. But I was pretty sure that even for $100 I would not be able to regain my lost erection.

James must have sensed that something was amiss. He turned around and saw my flaccid penis and the sack-like condom. Suddenly, he rose on all fours and whispered hoarsely, "Please, please fuck me now! Give it to me, Joseph! I know you can do it!" He moved his ass slowly from side to side.

His new pose, on his hands and knees, was much more evocative than the face-down position. Now he was like a submissive animal in heat inviting a dominant one to mount him. As I adjusted myself to align my dick with James's asshole, my wilted erection resurrected itself. I felt the condom stretching to accommodate my engorged penis. I knew that once I was deep inside James I could finish the job he had hired me for. Like a complete novice, without any probing, I thrust my cock into his ass as forcefully and as deeply as I could. He winced in pain. But now I was in a penetrator's heat, bent on coming inside him. I became oblivious of James' wants and needs. It was all about my ejaculation!

I don't know how long it took me to finish. It may have been just a minute. However short our mating, it was long enough for James. The moment I came, James, still on all fours, climaxed copiously. Fortunately, I had placed a beach towel in the center of the mattress earlier on. In this position, we collapsed on the bed with me still inside James.

Slowly, we disengaged. I removed the condom. For a brief interval we lay side by side, my arms around James's body. I thought he would be angry with me. I had fucked him like an inexperienced, horny teenager. "Joseph," he said softly, "this was *so* great. You're *so* wild."

Of course, my teenage-like ardor could be interpreted by James in only one way. He must have assumed that he had turned me on so much that, overwhelmed by my great passion, I reverted to a younger, more vigorous age. I wasn't going to tell him that for me it had all been an experiment. Had he not changed his position and through his own excitement gotten me hard again, I would have failed in my mission. I myself had experienced little physical pleasure from our encounter. But I was pleased that I had completed the experiment successfully and proved my own theory.

"I need to clean up a bit," I told James, and went to the bathroom. On the way, I grabbed my underwear. I wished to bring the session to a close. Not because I disliked him—I knew nothing about the man—but because it was time to end the charade. While I was washing up, I asked myself: Suppose James wants to make an appointment for next Thursday. What would I tell him? Suppose he would like to become my fuck buddy and see me *every* Thursday. Would I agree? After all, *I* make such arrangements with my sex workers all the time. But could *I* have sex with James once a week? True, this would "earn" me $50 per visit, $200 or more per month, depending on the number of Thursdays in a given thirty-day period. I looked at my watch. It was only 10:29. That was good pay for thirty minutes' work.

I returned to the sex room. James was sitting naked on the bed. When he saw that I had put on my underwear, he got the hint. He too started dressing. We didn't speak to each other. When he had all his clothes on, he looked at me quizzically. I understood what was going on in his mind. Seemingly, I had enjoyed our tryst, but now I was cold and distant, obviously wanting to be rid of him. Was he supposed to give me a kiss, embrace me, or just bid me a good day? In the end, totally confused, he mumbled, "See you around," and let himself out.

* * *

Suppose, just for the sake of the exercise, that James had really hired me as his sex worker. How did he fare?

First, James got the service that had been agreed upon. Whatever he had requested, from foreplay to penetration, was provided. At the end of the session he experienced a good orgasm. Though the worker's penetration technique left much to be desired, his intensity made up for it. When it was over, James was pleased by the worker's "wildness."

Second, for $50, James got a tremendous bargain. Michael and I have worked out a special financial arrangement between us. The price for in calls in San Francisco is around $100.

Third, the session took place in hygienic and pleasant surroundings. This is not always the case with in calls. In addition, safe(r) sex guidelines were adhered to by the worker.

Fourth, easy parking was available. Parking? Who cares about parking? Experienced clients who do in calls, that's who. Many sex workers and masseurs live downtown, where parking is a nightmare.

All in all, James received a good value for his money. But it was a pretty hollow experience. A physical connection occurred between worker and client, but they remained strangers to each other. It was merely an exchange of sex for money.

The following chapters are about exchanging sex for money and *much, much* more.

Chapter 1

Do Sex Workers Hustle
and Are Their Johns Clients?

Late in the evening of December 31, 1999, Gabriel, to whom I dedicated Chapter 10 in *A Consumer's Guide to Male Hustlers,* called to wish me a happy New Year. I was delighted to hear from him since I assumed that he had passed away. We had a long talk, bringing each other up to date. As an HIV-positive and clinically depressed person, Gabriel now lives under the welfare umbrella. He receives supplemental security income (SSI) funds, free medical care, and subsidized housing. He attends support groups and has even taken up spiritual practices such as yoga and meditation. Most important, he is finally clean and sober. Until he spoke to me, Gabriel had no idea that I had written a book about hustlers.

Gabriel had been my "regular" for some six years. Our conversation flowed easily. "Who is your hustler these days?" Gabriel asked.

"There are no hustlers in my life any longer."

"I don't believe you."

"They have been upgraded. They're now 'sex workers.' I see two workers interchangeably."

"Do you pay them more?"

"I have to. They're *professionals.*"

Gabriel chuckled. In his day, he had been the epitome of a good hustler as far as sexual performance was concerned. But he would never have made the grade as a professional sex worker. He had too many problems keeping appointments, and too many drastic mood swings while on assignment.

Only after we hung up did I calculate that nine years had passed since Gabriel and I were intimate. In my *Consumer's Guide,* I compare the work hustlers do to that of other independent contractors. Yet I have never received a social call from a dentist or a lawyer nine years after our professional relationship ended. More than money for services rendered must have existed between Gabriel and me. But what was it? Love? Certainly not. Sex? Gabriel was my type; I wasn't his. Friendship? We hadn't spoken to each other in many years. In Gabriel's case, it was shared intellectual interests and, despite his melancholy personality, a subtle sense of humor both of us enjoyed.

I write this to demonstrate the *nonsexual* intimacy I have achieved with quite a few of my hustlers. As far as I am concerned, the upgrade from "hustler" to "sex worker" is superfluous. As I will argue in later chapters, it may even be detrimental to the dynamics between workers and clients. But, regardless of my own feelings about this matter, we all have to keep up with the times.

By and large, sex workers who have read my *Consumer's Guide to Male Hustlers* liked the book. Understandably, all of them disapproved of my notion that they overcharge for their services. A few of them objected strongly to my usage of the term "hustler." They would have preferred "sex worker" or a euphemistic term such as "escort." Some even felt that "prostitute" was a more objective and less pejorative term.

I have enjoyed the services of hustlers for some four decades. The vast majority of my experiences have been positive. Naturally, I don't wish to offend this population. But I do have problems with alternative terms such as "sex worker," "escort," "call boy," "rent boy," and "prostitute."

The dictionary defines "hustler" as one who obtains money dishonestly. In colloquial usage, it refers to someone who is obsessed with making money any way possible, even if one has to cut corners to do so. So do hustlers hustle? Unfortunately, the answer to this simple question is quite complicated.

Saying that male sex work is an unregulated profession is an understatement. Any male, of any age, can prostitute himself. All he needs to do is ask for money in return for providing sex services. Unlike female sex workers who often find it difficult or even impossible to "unprostitute" themselves, males can do so with relative ease. Being able to "sex work" on a whim, it may even become a fun undertaking rather than hard work. It is easy to get started, because sex workers do not need to meet any qualifications. I will return to this last point often throughout the book.

Gays who are unfamiliar with the subject assume that sex workers must be good at what they do. After all, they are professionals. The truth is that some are good and some aren't. The ones who perform poorly may not be rehired—at least not by the same client. But in a large city, they can go through hundreds of clients before every potential trick has found out through a bad experience that they are poor performers. Then they can move to other cities and give poor service there. Some clients, including myself, will even train inexperienced hustlers because they are attracted to them and see a growth potential. In short, the fact that a guy decides to do sex work does not guarantee that he'll give good service.

Almost all sex workers hustle their clients in one way or another. The vast majority lie about their age (usually claiming to be younger—often *much* younger), and some even fib about their physical attributes and their ethnic mix.[1] The rationale behind lying is that a forty-five-year-old who can pass for thirty-five will satisfy the client just as well as one who is in his thirties. Unbeknownst to the hustler, his clients are rarely fooled. They simply don't tell him that they suspect his true age. This reinforces the hustler's belief that he does, indeed, look younger.

For instance, I met Ron through an ad in the San Francisco *Bay Area Reporter,* a gay publication. Ron described himself as a "cute & cuddly, youthful Amerasian." When I spoke to him on the phone, he told me that he was a nineteen-year-old Japanese American. When he arrived at my home, he looked cute enough, but he was obviously at least five years older than his stated age. He gave himself away as soon as he talked about himself. He simply had had too many experiences to fit into nineteen years.

When I opened the door, I had two options. Option one was to dismiss him for cause—that is, he had lied about his age. Option two: I could invite him in and thus indicate that we would proceed with the sex session. Practically speaking, the third option—telling Ron that I knew that he had lied about his age and then getting it on with him—wasn't open to me. We would have started off on the wrong foot.

As far as I was concerned, Ron was a responsive partner. As he had stated in his ad, he enjoyed cuddling and kissing thoroughly. He had a pleasant enough personality and was well educated. By the time we finished our first encounter, we were both pleased with the session. It made no sense for me to tell Ron that I knew that he was older than nineteen. Over a period of years we have seen each other some twenty-five times. Ron always holds decent jobs but likes to do sex work on the side; he needs the extra income because he parties a lot. He runs the same ad year after year. For the first three years of our acquaintanceship, his stated age in the ad was stuck at nineteen. One day when we were just chatting after our sex sessions, something Ron enjoys doing, I said to him conversationally, "Maybe it would be a good idea, Ron, if you moved your age up a bit in your ad."

He looked at me speculatively. "How old do you think I am?"

"I don't want to play guessing games. You advertised that you were nineteen when we first met. So now you must be twenty-two."

"No, really, Joseph, how old do you think I am?"

That was a no-win situation. Over the years, my silence about his age must have led him to believe that he looked much younger. How could I tell him now that I thought him to be about twenty-seven years old?

I deliberately erred on the young side. "You must be around twenty-five years old," I said.

"I'll be twenty-eight next month."

During the time I have know him, Ron has adjusted his age twice. At thirty years, he stated his age as twenty-two. He still advertises on a weekly basis. He is now around thirty-six and he advertises himself as a "youthful 24 y/o."

I assume that most of his clients are wise to him. So why do they put up with this hustle? (Of course, some don't, and dismiss him on the threshold.) I will deal with this point extensively in Chapter 12 when writing about "mature" sex workers. Suffice it to say here, once they sample Ron's versatile skills, they are pleased with him regardless of his true age. The long and short of it is that most sex workers will tell prospective clients whatever they want to hear. The rationale is always that the client is not really hurt by untruthfulness. Speaking metaphorically, sex workers do deliver the goods, even if the container is not exactly as stated. This way of conducting business is called hustling.

English, as well as many other languages, doesn't have a generic term for a male prostitute.[2] Not so many years ago, it would have been taken for granted that the term *prostitute* referred exclusively to a female. Even today, one must add "male" to "prostitute" to get the point across. Historically, *prostitute* has always been a pejorative term. *Female* prostitutes came up with the idea of upgrading the profession to sex work. Yet I have met quite a few male hustlers over the years who cheerfully described themselves as prostitutes. (Sometimes jokingly they use "ho," the folksy abbreviation of "whore.")

Personally, I would never say, "Tonight I'm meeting James, a male prostitute." It is an honest, earthy, and straightforward statement, but to me it sounds vulgar and pejorative. To say "Tonight I'm meeting James, a sex worker," sounds as exciting as a session with an accountant to prepare a tax return. Frankly, I have always felt comfortable with the term "hustler." It has a certain feel to it. Just a touch of adventure, illicitness, excitement, and lustfulness.

Long before the term *sex worker* came into being, hustlers referred to themselves, especially in ads, as escorts or models. The San Francisco gay publications, for instance, still list sex workers' advertisements under "Escorts and Models." Lately, the term *elite escorts* has gained currency.

The obvious problem with the terms *escort* and *model* is that they refer to two vocations that—theoretically—have no connection whatsoever with sex work. In my particular case, these terms also make no sense at all. I have never paid a sex worker to escort me anywhere, nor did I ever hire anyone to model for me. My regular sex worker, Michael, to whom I devoted the last chapter of the *Consumer's Guide,* refers to his work as "escorting." (As opposed to the bad old days when, in his words, he was "a street hustler.") Sometimes, when I call him, I will ask, "Can you escort me next Friday?" Michael has many sterling qualities, but a sense of humor is not one of them. He doesn't see anything funny in my questions even though, over a period of three years, he and I have been out in public only once, for a cup of coffee.

I ran into the term *elite escorts* for the first time in Matt Adams' book *Hustlers, Escorts, Porn Stars.*[3] The term immediately trickled down into sex workers' ads. Now some advertise themselves as "elite escorts." I don't know who authorizes them to bestow upon themselves this exalted title, but I can understand why Adams considers porn stars to be elite escorts.

The much-maligned street hustler has one advantage over all sex workers who advertise their services. He is in plain view of the buyer. The more scant the hustler's clothing, the more informed the buyer's selection can be. This is why guys on the street often wear nothing more than a T-shirt even on the coldest nights. By contrast, when a sex worker describes himself over the phone, he can convey only an approximation of what he is all about. Even the most precise and truthful information does not come close to eyeballing. A photograph in an ad, even a recent one, is a static document. However, a film is a dynamic record, giving the buyer a precise, almost in vivo, impression of the person. Buyers of sex services who seek physically perfect partners are willing to pay extremely high rates for porn stars whose faces, bodies, and sexual prowess they have witnessed on film. Added to this is the veneration in which so many gays hold these stars. In his book about the late gay porn star Joey Stefano, Charles Isherwood writes: "Porn stars . . . are thus the only gay movie stars."[4] Being able to engage in sex with a *star* is worth a bundle! In this context, "elite escort" makes more sense.

It has been my experience that clients who are type oriented (for instance, boy next door, blue collar, athletic, black, Asian, Hispanic, androgynous) are more likely to be satisfied when selecting sex workers from advertisements than clients who seek perfection in their partners. Perversely, the perfection seekers are more likely to be disappointed, even when they finally find exactly what they have been looking for. In the short run, visually perfect specimens often have a bad attitude because they have an inflated opinion of themselves. In the long run, in the presence of perfection, a client is likely to attempt to overlook a lot of bad character traits. After a while, if the physically perfect sex worker has a lousy personality, it will become too irritating to ignore.

The terms "call boy" and especially "rent boy" are not without merit as alternative designations to hustlers, but they also bring unwanted baggage with them. The word "boy" is problematic for a number of reasons: first, because in English the usage of *boy* tends to denigrate an adult addressed in this fashion; second, because it implies sex with minors; third, because it is ridiculous to refer to a six-feet-four-inch, 200-pound athlete in his late thirties as a "boy."

We are back to square one. The designation "hustler" for a man selling sex may be the most descriptive term. Nevertheless, from now on, I'll use the term "sex worker" except where the noun "hustler" is more appropriate. I'll also use "hustler" when writing about earlier times when all sex workers were known as hustlers. I will not sacrifice historical accuracy on the altar of political correctness.

In addition to political correctness, another reason exists that some hustlers deserve an upgrade in their status. Real professionalism has started to make inroads into this vocation. I believe that this new professionalism is due to three completely unrelated developments.

Conducting one's sex business from one's home rather than from the street requires constant advertising. In the late 1960s, gay publications started to flourish.[5] They welcomed sex workers' advertisements both for income and to satisfy their readers' curiosity. (Many gays who never engage sex workers are regular readers of these ads.) In time, the publications categorized these advertisements in a logical order. They even weeded out con artists, common in those early days, by refusing to run their ads. This allowed sex workers to move their business off the streets.

It was the pager that made it possible for sex workers to conduct their business twenty-four hours a day. Now they could leave their homes and still respond to clients' calls immediately. Even sex workers who had no permanent address could advertise their services. All they needed was a pager and a public telephone to return the calls.

The fitness craze that has dominated the gay community for approximately the past two decades has motivated an enormous number of gays to work out at gyms.[6] The preferred look in the gay community nowadays is that of a man spending a considerable amount of time on exercise machines. A sex worker who is a "gym rat" will command a better fee. With the gyms came personal trainers, special diets, expensive supplements, and sometimes even anabolic steroids. Sex workers who work hard and spend good money to shape their bodies and enhance their appearance have made a real investment in the success of their business.[7] With a substantial business investment and *future* prospects, male sex workers have begun to consider their work a real profession.

In *A Consumer's Guide,* I quoted John Preston's *Hustling: A Gentleman's Guide to the Fine Art of Homosexual Prostitution,* on a number of occasions.[8] His book is a how-to manual for sex workers who want to go into business for themselves. This is a very different approach from the guys in earlier times who stood on the streets trying to pick up a trick. They had zero investment in the business. All they wanted was to make a quick buck; professionalism was the least of their concerns. I hasten to add here that professionalism does not guarantee a better sex session. The quality of the sexual encounter depends on the innate skills, experience, and attitude of the sex worker. Professionalism brings about better grooming, keeping appointments, and, most important, not cutting corners during the session. It *almost* always guarantees the client an all-around safe session. Like any other businessman, an established sex worker must build and maintain his reputation.

We now come to the term *client* versus *john* and *trick*. In his book, Matt Adams writes:

> It is frowned upon in the areas of modeling, bodybuilding, and dancing to engage in escort work even though it is very common. That is why people in these jobs that engage in escort work are very discrete [sic]. A hustler has customers, an escort has clients, and these elite escorts have sponsors.[9]

"Client" sounds better than "customer" and is certainly more flattering than "john" or "trick." But Matt Adams notwithstanding, the relationship between client and his service provider is not based on the elegance or the affluence of the former but rather on the obligations of the latter. Not only lawyers and accountants have clients; social workers serving the homeless also refer to them as clients. The interests of the client, at least in theory, are paramount and take precedence over those of the server. Ideally, the obligation of a lawyer is to provide the best possible service to his client *regardless* of whether it also serves the former's interests. As we all know, in real life, whether in lawyering or in sex work, things are never so straightforward.

My objection to Adams' definitions is not only on semantic grounds. The fact that a porn star operates from a beautifully furnished apartment and has sex with Silicon Valley options millionaires doesn't change the nature of the transaction. The street hustler who gets screwed by a drunk in an alley for the price of a bottle of booze performs essentially the same service. The only difference is in the setting and the compensation. (Referring to female prostitutes, George Bernard Shaw made this observation long before Matt Adams wrote his book.)

But just as I changed my terminology from hustler to sex worker, I will keep using client rather than customer, john, or trick, unless one of the three terms seem to be more appropriate in a certain instance.

Chapter 2

Agencies, the Internet, and Advance Bookings

AGENCIES

In *A Consumer's Guide to Male Hustlers,* I have discussed sex workers' agencies only in passing. I have always believed that agency workers do not fit the definition of independent contractors. They are more similar to employees than to autonomous operators. But I have been asked by a number of readers to describe these agencies more fully. The following is a brief discussion of this subject.

The function of sex workers' agencies is to find suitable escorts for their clients and facilitate meetings between the parties. (An agency is not a whorehouse. Sometimes, though, it serves as a house for in calls and as an agency for out calls.) For this service, the agency takes a cut of the fee paid by the client to the worker. On the average, the cut is about 40 percent of the total fee. Most agencies charge an additional fee of an equal amount for every sixty minutes after the first hour. To make sure this happens, agencies usually require the escort to check in when he arrives at the client's home or hotel and once again when the session is over. This tends to create an artificial rush. If the client must pay double the fee precisely after one hour, he will be more likely to make sure that he climaxes well before the hour is over.

How do clients benefit from paying the agency's high fees? It saves them the tedious and often frustrating task of going through sex workers' ads and setting up appointments. This is an important consideration, especially when clients find themselves in a city they don't know well, stay at hotels on the outskirts, or are pressed for time.

All the other benefits for the client are iffy. To understand why, we must look at how agencies conduct their business. The agencies' main problem is that they have no way of predicting ahead of time how busy they will be on a given night or what sort of workers will be in demand. When agencies cannot come up with the perfect worker for the client, they will substitute the next best available. Clients who make reservations well ahead of time are much more likely to get the most suitable workers.

When an agency engages a worker, it makes sure that he is presentable, well groomed, and displays a pleasant personality. Agencies also ask their workers about their sexual proclivities. For instance, are they tops, bottoms, or versatile? Most agencies do not test their workers—that is, conduct a trial session. A few do, which workers invariably resent, because they do not get paid for them.

Obviously, agencies providing sexual services, an illegal activity, are not in a position to run security checks on their employees. Usually, they also do not perform health checks. So is hiring an agency worker safer than someone chosen from a newspaper? The answer is simple. The longer a worker has been with an agency, the safer he is likely to be. Workers handle relatively large sums of money before they make their "drop"—that is, when they hand over the agency's cut to the proprietor. Long-term workers prove their reliability by bringing in the agency's cut punctually and faithfully. Also, they would not have lasted with an agency if complaints had been filed against them.

Clients are probably somewhat safer with workers sent out by an agency than the ones they choose from an ad in the paper or on the Internet. However, if for political reasons the district attorney or the police decide to bust male escorts who advertise their services, they'll get more bang for their buck going after agencies than after individuals. One agency could yield many workers and, worse, the names and personal data of its clients.

All agencies are faced with similar logistical problems. On one hand, they must have many workers on their rosters to cater to a variety of tastes, and in case they are swamped with calls. On the other hand, they can have only a few workers standing by—giving up their entire night to the agency. As a result, some workers must see two or three clients in a span of a few hours without time for recuperation.

In *A Consumer's Guide* I argue against tipping sex workers. They are independent professionals and charge a pretty dollar for their services. This is less true for sex workers employed by agencies who have to kick back the agency's large cut. As a result, clients are expected to factor in an appropriate tip. The tipping is made awkward by agencies who require the client to pay at the beginning of the session. It hardly makes sense to tip a worker *before* a service has been rendered. Once clients have paid for the session up front, they are less likely to provide a tip at the end.

The greatest fear of agency owners is that a deal will be struck between clients and workers for future calls, eliminating the agency altogether. For example, Omar, whom I profile in Chapter 10, worked briefly for an escort agency. While he was an employee of the agency, he also ran his own ads. On one occasion, when he was sent on a call, it turned out to be a client whom he had already met through his own ad. Naturally, the client felt that the agency was an unnecessary redundancy. He made Omar an offer he couldn't refuse. In the future, he would see Omar without going through the agency. This would save the client the agency's fee, which he was willing to split with Omar. Both client and worker came out winners. Agency owners are justifiably afraid of this kind of scenario, but there is little they can do about it.

Being on the roster of a busy agency has one tremendous advantage for sex workers. Screening phone calls is often more stressful to them than the sex session itself. Workers have to deal with jerk-off calls, crackpots, window shoppers, and mischief makers. (The last set up dates for addresses that do not exist.) Furthermore, efficiently handling phone calls from strangers requires skills that many sex workers do not have. Some workers are willing to earn less through an agency to avoid the endless ringing of the phone.

For many reasons, it is rare for a worker to last long with an agency. For the vast majority of workers, the whole point of "escorting" is to be free from bosses and the rules of the workplace. Agency workers are subjected to many rules, feel that the percentage taken out of their fee is excessive, and disagree with proprietors. Agencies almost always promise workers to provide more calls than they can deliver. Typically, though not always, agencies are more attractive to novice sex workers who "apprentice" with them for a while and then become independent.

As far as the buyer is concerned, agencies are at their best with repeat clients and when given advance notice. They are also useful (though dizzyingly expensive) for clients living in rural areas. Agencies oblige their workers to watch the clock punctiliously. For well-heeled clients, it is probably more satisfying physically and emotionally to engage workers for the whole night. It helps make the experience more relaxing and harmonious. For workers, it provides a harder but more lucrative assignment.

SEX WORKERS ADVERTISING ON THE WEB

Sex workers have many advantages when advertising their services on the Web (see the Appendix). Often, the ads are free. Even paid advertisements are cheaper on the Web than in printed media. Clients contact workers via e-mail, thus cutting down on telephone inquiries. Out-of-town clients can get in touch with workers to make appointments for future dates. Unfortunately, some freaks lurk the Internet who play e-mail jerk-off games. They engage workers in steamy correspondence with no intention of ever meeting them in person.

Arguably, clients who use computers are more prosperous and sophisticated than the ones who choose their workers through newspaper ads. This gives escorts and masseurs advertising their services on the Web an excuse to impose an "Internet surcharge." Invariably, masseurs and escorts quote higher rates on the Web than in printed ads.

To corroborate the last point, I asked subscribers to a sex workers' mailing list how they regarded online clients. Here is one worker's reply:

> When I advertised in newspapers and magazines, I charged a flat rate of $100 per hour for my services. Now that I have become established on the Internet, I charge a flat rate of $150 per hour. I have noticed, in addition, that the class of clients has changed drastically. I think it could be due to the fact that people who own and can operate a computer tend to be more educated and wealthier. I could be wrong, but that adds an unexpected bonus for those sex workers using the Internet to advertise.

Workers advertising on the Web prefer exchanging e-mails to talking on the phone. This does not necessarily serve the interests of the client. Interviewing a worker on the phone gives a much more accurate impression of what he is all about. However, some clients, especially the married ones, also prefer the anonymity of the Internet to giving out their phone numbers.

Most workers display a photo with their ad when they advertise on the Web. Those who do not should be willing to send it as an e-mail attachment. The excuse "I don't have a jpg" is unacceptable. If the advertiser is sophisticated enough to get on a sex workers' Web site, he should be able to find a way to scan his photo or use a digital camera. Just as in the printed media, the digital image is not date stamped; it may be ancient history.

Throughout this book, I emphasize the enormous advantages of making dates ahead of time rather than on the spur of the moment. Using the Internet prevents last-minute meetings which, in my opinion, serves both worker and client well.

As far as clients are concerned, escorts who advertise their services on the Internet do not automatically make better sex workers. No correlation whatsoever exists between computer literacy and good sex work. Unless it serves a specific purpose (for instance, booking a worker in a distant city), financially frugal clients will probably do better for themselves if they search sex workers' ads in gay papers.

But, in my opinion, advertising on the Web will soon become the norm. For advertisers, the Web has the advantage of being low or no cost. With more people having access to the Internet, ads placed on various Web sites will be seen by more potential clients. Lately, this trend has become obvious: Many personal ad columns in gay publications (for relationships as well as for sex work) have become shorter over the past few years. Advertisers have been transferring their business from print to cyberspace. In desperation, some publications have even started featuring ads twice in the same column to make it appear a bit longer.

ADVANCE BOOKING VERSUS SPONTANEITY

In *A Consumer's Guide* (Chapter 11), I described a monthly arrangement with a hustler. I committed myself to seeing him ten times a month; in return, he charged me much less than the going rate. It turned out to be a bad idea. Instead of an independent contractor, I had a disgruntled employee on my hands. I did not repeat this mistake with Michael, my regular. He and I do not have a contract to see each other at given intervals, but I am his *very* regular "regular." This status confers privileges and imposes obligations on both parties.

Michael gives me "a most-favorite client" rate. I make enough monthly appointments with him to allow him to count on me as a steady source of income. We are both bound by the same code of honor. Once we have made an appointment, I don't break it even if I can get a freebie; he doesn't wriggle out, even if a better-paying client requests an appointment in my time slot. During our entire association, he called in sick only three times, and I canceled once due to illness.

I have been asked often by readers how such advance bookings affect spontaneity. I'll end this chapter with an anecdote to illustrate how this plays out in real life.

Since arriving in San Francisco thirty-six years ago, I have always celebrated my birthdays by utilizing the services of a sex worker. The only exceptions were birthdays when I had a lover. A sex worker on one's *birthday?* How terribly sad and lonely the author must be! No, neither sad nor lonely; rather, experienced in the ways of gay life. The chances of being stood up for a sex date are at least 50 percent. If the appointment is made a week ahead of time (say, with one's birthday in mind), the chances of the prospective partner flaking out could run as high as 90 percent. Stuff (not to use the more vulgar four-letter word) always seems to happen to make it impossible for the other fellow to keep his appointment. With sex workers of long standing, things usually *do* work out. Between taking my chances on a birthday of *maybe* picking up the hunkiest man in a bar for free or paying for an even ordinary-looking sex worker, I have always opted for the latter.

April 1996, was an important time in my life. I would celebrate my sixty-fifth birthday at the end of the month. At the beginning of the year, I had lost my regular sex worker, forcing me to employ "temps" until I could find a suitable replacement. The particular escort I engaged for my birthday was Oscar, about whom I will write much more in Chapter 6. By 1996, we had known each other for some eight years. Oscar, of Hispanic and African-American descent, was not the most handsome escort, but both of us were fiercely attracted to each other sexually; emotionally, we had a complicated and ambivalent relationship. Oscar always had a big chip on his shoulder when dealing with me.

Over the years, I had trained Oscar, a former street hustler, to keep his appointments with me. In April 1996, he worked as a caregiver for a person with AIDS (PWA), in a dangerous San Francisco neighborhood. The deal was that on my birthday I would pick him up at six o'clock, when he got off work. Once we were done, I would return him to his own place, located in an equally dismal neighborhood.

For my birthday, a friend had invited me to lunch downtown. I left my car in the Castro and went downtown by public transportation. On the way back, around two in the afternoon, I was waiting for the light to change at 18th and Castro Streets. A driver made a right turn against the light, almost hitting a pedestrian. It was a close call. I muttered something about San Francisco drivers to the guy standing next to me. We crossed the street together. I noticed that he kept looking at me. I took him to be a Hispanic man in his early thirties. He appeared pleasant enough, although I wasn't particularly attracted to him. As we walked along Castro, he said, "You know, you're really cute."

"Well, thank you very much. That's just what I needed to hear today."

"Why today?"

"It's my sixty-fifth birthday."

"Happy birthday! May I kiss you?"

In San Francisco's Castro District, kissing wasn't a big deal. "That's the best offer I've had today. Please do."

It was far from a chaste birthday kiss. I took it as the first step in the mating ritual. Too bad that I have a date with Oscar at six, I thought. I won't have time for my new admirer. But it is my birthday! And not just an ordinary birthday—a milestone event. All during April, I've been worrying about my new status. In my autumn years, how would I fare in the youth-oriented gay culture? Bringing back a trophy to my lair on this day of all days would be proof that my sexual prowess is still intact. Quickly, I made up my mind. I would take the stranger home and deal with Oscar later. "What is your name?" I asked the man who had just kissed me.

"Manuel."

"I'm Joseph. Now that you've kissed me on the street, may I invite you home to . . . talk a bit more?"

"Where do you live?"

"A mile uphill from here. My car is parked two blocks away. Do you have a car?"

"Yes. I'll follow you."

Driving home, I reflected on what had just happened. The last time I had been picked up on the street was in the late 1960s. But that was then. Now, as a novice senior citizen, was it wise for me to let strangers into my home? Why was it happening to me today, of all days? Oh, well, I thought, with a shorter life expectancy I could afford to take more chances. My new motto should be *carpe diem*! I looked in the rearview mirror. Manuel was following me in his station wagon. The windshield of his vehicle displayed an airline decal.

When we arrived at my house, I asked Manuel whether I could make him a cup of coffee. "Let me be frank with you," he said. "I really want to have sex with you, but I'm in a bit of a hurry. This morning my lover and I flew in from Quito, Ecuador. I need to get home and get ready for work."

"You flew in from Quito? You have a lover?"

"We both work for the same airline. He lives in Seattle. We commute back and forth. I work at the airport here. And I *love* older men."

"How old is your lover?"

"He is only five years older than me. I'm thirty-three. I wish he were older. But that's another story."

"Well, I haven't had a quickie in a long time. Let's get on with it."

Manuel was a good sex partner and the quickie took longer than I expected. Resting with Manuel nestled in my arms after both of us had climaxed, I realized that the Universe was sending me a message. It proclaimed unequivocally, "Go on with your 'sexcapades' as heretofore. The best is yet to come."

It was close to four o'clock when Manuel left me. I was sexually fulfilled, spiritually rejuvenated, and physically spent. What the hell was I going to do about my date with Oscar? I had no desire to see him, much less pick him up and have sex with him. But I had made a commitment to him. My word has always been my bond.

I dozed off for a while. When I woke, it was close to six. Much too late to pick Oscar up. I called him at work. His patient, as well as Oscar, liked to play loud music. I had to shout to be heard. "I'm sorry, Oscar, I can't make it this afternoon."

"What did you say?"

"I can't make it today," I said very slowly and loudly. "I'll call you tomorrow morning." The next day would be Oscar's day off. I would call him at home. I hung up the phone.

When I called Oscar the next morning, he was furious. I told him exactly what had happened to me the previous day. When I finished, he said, "Sounds pretty shady to me."

"Well, I can prove it."

"How?"

"You know that I'm a writer, maybe not a great one, but even a first-year student taking up creative writing would have come up with a better plot than the story I've just told you. It's such a cockamamie tale that it *must* be true."

"Don't call me a cocksucker, Joseph!" Oscar said threateningly. His high-pitched voice bordered on hysterical.

"Who's calling you a cocksucker?"

"You just said 'cocksomething.'"

He was not the most educated of sex workers. "Oscar, I said 'cockamamie.' It means—never mind what it means. All I am saying is that had I wanted to lie to you, I would have come up with a better story."

"You're right about that. It's a stupid story." In the end, Oscar believed me. In his experience, I had never stood him up. "So when will I see you?"

"I'll pick you up from work the day after tomorrow."

If the pattern of being picked up on the streets every thirty years holds, I won't have to worry about another such incident until I am well into my nineties! I am positive that had it not been the most special day in my life, my sixty-fifth birthday, I would have tried to postpone my meeting with Manuel for another time and kept my appointment with Oscar. Experience tells me that I would have missed my only chance with Manuel. Doubtless, some spontaneity is lost when one makes appointments with sex workers in advance. But I am happier with the rigidity of scheduling sex workers ahead of time rather than waiting for free sex partners to proposition me on the street.

Chapter 3

Tarred by the Straight Brush

Chapter 3 of my last book is titled, "Hustling—a Vocation?" In that chapter I wrote that a natural vocation for prostitution is essential to be a successful male sex worker. Many sex workers share my opinion.[1] I will add here that feeling good about the job is equally important. But instead of me expounding on this subject, I'll let sex workers speak for themselves. In a 1992 video, produced in San Francisco, five local escorts were interviewed.[2] The producer chose escorts ranging from nineteen to "old," from cute to unappealing, and from various ethnic groups.

Escort Franco speaks for all of them when he says, "If you don't have the right attitude, [escorting] will become a drag." Steve, in my eyes the cutest of them all and no longer in the escort business, has a bad attitude. "I'd never hustle again," he says. "[It] drags me down. [It makes] me feel subservient . . . and dirty." On the other hand, Vic, an older man, asserts that escorting has made him into a "great diplomat, an actor, a service provider." As an escort he has had the "best time of my life." John, who is HIV positive and appears to be ill during the interview, sees no future in escorting. The video ends with a question directed to him: "Why are you participating in this film?" With a wan smile, he answers, "I'm repenting."

What makes this somewhat amateurish video so fascinating are the unexpected incongruities. For instance, the older escorts are happier with their work than the younger ones are. While cute Steve feels subservient and dirty, the more mature Franco feels empowered and in control at all times. Rafael, an aging "bear," considers sex work as a balm for his ego.

It has always been my contention that both workers and clients are influenced in their attitudes not only by their own feelings and experiences, but also by how gay society regards them. Rick Whitaker's *Assuming the Position: A Memoir of Hustling,* is all about self-loathing because of external prejudices.[3] With commendable frankness, the author describes himself during his hustling days as a drug addict, an alcoholic, and a shoplifter. In this state, all he could possibly do to earn a living, and a very decent one at that, was to hustle. The challenge for most escorts, especially beginners, is immediately to turn themselves on sexually upon entering the home of a complete stranger. Uniquely, Whitaker performs well in such situations. He writes, "I am always better in bed with a stranger than with someone I particularly like. . . ."[4]

Here we have a man who has no choice but to prostitute himself (if he wants to continue his drug habit), who is superbly skilled at his calling, and even enjoys it, *and* who is money hungry. "The money, of course, is the trump. An escort is always paid in untaxed cash, and I almost never worked for less than $150 an hour . . . this aspect of hustling was thrilling . . . for someone such as myself who has never had much money."[5]

Whitaker describes vividly how good he is at playing various sexual roles and how grateful his clients are for his services. But, inexplicably, Whitaker is unhappy with his lot. It is not quite obvious to readers what Whitaker's problem is, because he does not give personal reasons for wanting to give up hustling. Instead, to explain his existential dilemma, he relies on three famous philosophers to argue his case. In a brief final chapter, he refers extensively to Nietzche, Thoreau, and Wittgenstein to make clear to himself why he should give up hustling. (I am jealous of Whitaker's clients. None of *my* sex workers has been familiar with the works of all three philosophers.) My take is that what bothers Whitaker is not the sex work per se. By and large, straight as well as gay society believes axiomatically that prostitution is harmful physically, psychologically, and spiritually. Whitaker buys into these prejudices.

It takes great courage to ignore the social and "scientific" harangues against male prostitution, even for a practitioner who is perfectly happy with his work. For instance, a while ago I attended a San Francisco reading by Matt Bernstein Sycamore, promoting a book he edited, in which twenty-four sex workers write about their clients.[6] Matt related that he "sex worked" in each city he visited to cover his expenses while touring the country. At one bookstore, a female social worker came up to him after the reading and said, "You know that when sex workers stop prostituting themselves, they *always* suffer from post-traumatic stress syndrome."

Matt and all other male escorts must have a lot of inner strength not to buy into the guilt trip society lays on them.

Like so many other escorts, Whitaker does not much appreciate the hands that feed him. He describes his johns as lonely men for whom he sometimes feels sorry. The rest of the time he criticizes them. Bitchily, he even derides their decor and deplores their musical tastes. The johns for whom Whitaker provided services were all wealthy men. (They had to be to afford Whitaker's agencies' high fees.) Presumably, most of them have made their fortunes by using their brains. So why are these men hiring escorts such as Whitaker, instead of going to bars and sex clubs or becoming sugar daddies?

The obvious answer is that for some wealthy and intelligent clients, hiring escorts for casual sex is more satisfying than rubbing shoulders with a multitude of strangers at sex clubs, wasting their time at unbearably noisy bars, or catering to the capricious whims of spoiled "sugar sons." Because they have the money and the smarts, they get to have sex with skillful escorts such as Rick Whitaker. But unless these clients have been hiring sex workers from the beginning of their gay careers, they are just as unlikely as Whitaker to be happy with their roles. Consciously or unconsciously, we gays are guided by straight social mores. Our attitudes toward male prostitution reflect the straight attitude toward the female variety. By gay society's norms, it is far nobler for a cruiser to spend untold hours at an upscale bar, waste his money buying drinks for middling potential partners, and finally take home as his trophy a soused runt rather than engage the services of the pleasure provider of his choice.

The following vignette is a poignant illustration of the gay bias toward sex workers. In *A Consumer's Guide to Male Hustlers* (p. 38), I describe Jerry Elgin, an exceptionally intelligent and good-looking hustler, who studied French at San Francisco City College and planned to visit Paris the following summer. Jerry was one of my regulars for a while. We also became good friends.

This was in the 1970s, when I still went to bathhouses at least once a week both to save money and face. I had to prove to myself that I could get sex for free. On one such occasion, I met Marcel at a bathhouse and had sex with him. He was a handsome, young French tourist. Jerry and I had planned on going to the gay nude beach at San Gregorio the following Sunday. It occurred to me that Marcel also might enjoy an outing to the nude beach. Jerry would benefit from meeting Marcel by establishing a future contact in Paris. I invited Marcel to come with us, and he accepted.

Jerry brought a friend along. There were four of us in my car. With the chronically foggy weather along this coast, San Gregorio is rarely warm enough to cavort comfortably in the nude. But on this particular Sunday in October, the weather was perfect, the gay crowd was playful, and we all had a good time. Jerry and Marcel got along well. They made a matching pair: young, graceful, and intelligent. I was pleased when I observed them flirting with each other. It would be good for Jerry to have Marcel in Paris to guide him. However, when it was almost time to leave, Marcel took me aside and asked in great agitation, "Do you know that Jerry is a hustler?" In Marcel's charming French accent, hustler became *hustlair.*

"*Bien sûr, mon cher ami,*" I answered jovially, though I was really upset. Had Jerry's friend opened his big mouth and told Marcel that Jerry was a *hustlair?*

"I can't speak to a *hustlair,*" said Marcel.

"Oh, yes, you can. You've been talking to him all day."

"I don't *wish* to speak to Monsieur Jerry Elgin!"

Calling Jerry *monsieur* was not meant to honor him but, rather, to distance Marcel from the *hustlair.*

"Did Monsieur Elgin propose sex to you in exchange for money?"

"Of course not."

"Then I don't understand your problem."

Marcel was offended by my answer. He reflected for a moment and said: "I'm surprised and disappointed that an educated man like you would have friends who are . . . prostitutes." After this pronouncement, Marcel turned away and sulked.

Our drive back to San Francisco was awkward for all of us. Palpable tension existed in the car—all the more so because Jerry and Marcel sat next to each other in the backseat, as they had done earlier in the day. With a barely audible *merci* and *adieu,* Marcel took his French leave as I stopped in front of his hotel.

It turned out that it was Jerry himself who had told Marcel that he was a hustler. Because all my friends knew and accepted Jerry as my hustler and buddy, he assumed that Marcel too would not be put off by his part-time occupation.

As I wrote in *A Consumer's Guide,* Jerry looked forward to hustling in Paris as the greatest challenge and adventure of his trip. It would test to the limit both his skills as a sex worker and his newly acquired knowledge of French. But of course he wasn't going to proposition Marcel. The abrupt change of attitude on Marcel's part, from flirtatious to contemptuous, was a reflection of the low esteem hustlers are accorded by gay society. In this attitude, Marcel mirrored the feelings of straights toward female prostitutes.

The title *Assuming the Position* is clever, but it does not represent Whitaker's own experiences nor, indeed, those of most *male* sex workers. In the video I mentioned earlier, the meekest of the escorts, John the Repentant, states that he would allow clients to screw him but he would never blow a client. (Such quirky preferences are discussed at length in *A Consumer's Guide,* pp. 92-93.) How subservient are escorts if they can unilaterally decide which positions they will assume during the sex session?

Sex workers feel sorry for themselves because gay society has determined that they are despicable. Many of their clients pity themselves for having to resort to hustlers' services. The workers, in turn, pity their own clients for being "lonely" and not being able to do better for themselves than seek out prostitutes.

All jobs, especially well-paying ones, have their unique dangers and stresses. In the video, Steve discusses the dangers an escort faces from unhinged johns.[7] At nineteen years of age, Steve could have been a rookie policeman. As a cop, he would have spent his entire day knowing that he could be shot and killed by an enraged driver objecting to a traffic citation.

But aren't sex workers often driven into prostitution because of economic hardships? In this case, they certainly would have good reasons to feel sorry for themselves. I know the answer to this question because I have observed it in the United States and abroad for a long time. I'll give two illustrations to show that the need for money does sometimes drive men into prostitution, but that it is only *one* of many other options open to them.

Many young and single Mexicans cross into the United States illegally and work here for a while as an adventure. For some of these guys, it can be a rite of passage more than an economic necessity. (It is generally the somewhat older, married men who have to do it to provide for their families.) In the 1960s and 1970s, when I used to pick up street hustlers on Polk Street in San Francisco, I would run into gay Mexicans and other Hispanics who were in this country without papers. That they zeroed in on Polk Street right away and, in spite of their extremely limited English, managed to go into business as hustlers never ceased to amaze me. Once these guys discovered that I was fluent in Spanish, I was upgraded immediately from a gringo trick to *un amigo de confianza*—a confidant.

José Luis was one of the many Latin American hustlers on Polk Street. I liked him a lot. He was a *jarocho,* one of the natives of the state of Veracruz on the Caribbean coast of Mexico. José Luis was short with a dark complexion and his black hair was very thick. Unlike most street hustlers, he was well organized, punctual, and had his own phone. It was easy to make dates with him rather than having to search for him on the street. José Luis regarded himself as gay. From the very beginning of his stay here, he supported himself by hustling. Since he didn't do drugs, he made enough money to pay his rent, feed himself, buy nice clothes, and send some money to his family back home.

One day his cousin Pablo crossed the border from Tijuana, in Baja California. The next day he arrived at José Luis's tiny apartment. Unlike José Luis, his cousin was straight. Just as José Luis had known where to hustle, his cousin knew where he could find work. In San Francisco, as in most other cities in California, undocumented workers offer their services as day laborers in a well-defined area. There they mill around every morning until they are chosen by employers who give them work for a day or for a week. They are paid a low wage for very hard work. Like street hustlers, they face many unpleasant situations, including being paid less than the agreed-upon wage—or not at all—or being busted by the *migra* and deported to Mexico (only to be back at very same corner a few days later).

Pablo was much more handsome than his cousin. In my presence, José Luis teased him. *"Dedícate a la prostitución,"* he told him, "and you'll make good money. You have a nice body and your face isn't too bad." But Pablo chose the hardships of day labor because nothing was gay about him. He could no more work as a male escort than gay José Luis could have made money by working as a gigolo servicing women. Of course, José Luis hustled to survive. But other work was available to him.

I have had sex in the Philippines with *certifiable* straights, married men with children—highly prized by some wealthy Filipino gays.[8] They were poor and they did prostitute themselves for the extra income, but I never felt that they were doing something that violated their sexual integrity. It seemed to me that they were enjoying the worshipful adulation and, of course, the pesos lavished on them by their *baklâ* (queer) patrons. In my case, to all appearances, they were also enjoying themselves *physically*. Unlike Pablo, they were truly bisexual. Their heterosexual nature begot them children; their homosexual side helped them earn extra money.

One complaint voiced by many sex workers is that their job interferes with their own sexuality. Three of the escorts in the previously mentioned video complain about enormous difficulty in switching gears when dating (as opposed to escorting). They have a valid point. The irony is that the *less* sex work they do, the easier the "switching of gears." This is why the libido of part-time workers is much less affected by their job. The 24/7 workers suffer the most because, physically and psychologically, they have no opportunity to recuperate. Aaron Lawrence describes this dilemma accurately and entertainingly.[9]

> In Summation: Only sex workers who have a vocation for their calling and a positive attitude toward their profession, are comfortable with themselves and what they have to do to make money. And only clients who appreciate the enormous advantages of engaging sex workers over cruising for *casual* sex, do not end up berating themselves for consorting with prostitutes.

Another antihustler process is going on in the gay community, which probably does not have a counterpart among straights and female prostitutes. I believe that it is related to the ability of sex workers to "hustlerize" and "unhustlerize" themselves in a blink of an eye.

The best anecdote I can use to illustrate this point is an experience I had at a Toronto bathhouse in 1999. After many years of absence, I visited the city I had once made my home. The trip had two purposes: to visit old friends and to promote *A Consumer's Guide*. These activities kept me quite busy, especially in the evenings. Even if I had wanted to, I wouldn't have had the time to go to the bars or to cruise.

Bringing sex workers to my hotel was out of the question. For some strange reason, the hotel I stayed at—part of an international chain—didn't have safe deposit boxes in the rooms or at the reception desk. Because I was selling copies of my book, I had a lot of cash on hand. I wasn't going to violate my own safety rules set out in *A Consumer's Guide* (p. 141).

My gay friends in Toronto told me of a local bathhouse that usually kept sex workers in circulation. This seemed an ideal solution: safe, efficient, and sanitary. It was a pleasant enough bathhouse. No sooner did I shower than I was approached by a sex worker called Ted. He was young, slightly hairy, a tad on the heavy side, and as fair as they come. His blond hair was arranged in a neat, long pony tail. Ted was a newcomer to Toronto. His home was in Charlottetown, the capital of Prince Edward Island. Though quite good looking, he was definitely not my physical type. I was also somewhat turned off by the metal stud in his tongue. We chatted for a while and then, not to waste his time, I told him, "You're a very nice guy, but, unfortunately, not my type. I like darker men."

But as I said this, my body sent out a strong signal belying my statement. It was so strong that Ted must have noticed it. After all, I had only a towel draped around my waist. Well, I thought, why not do something different on my vacation? Ted would be a completely new experience in my life. I had never had sex with a native of Prince Edward Island, Canada's smallest province. "See, Ted, men can't lie. My dick just informed me that you *are* my type."

We agreed on forty dollars, and I invited him to my room. His fee seemed low, but an awful lot of free competition existed in the bathhouse. He was extremely affectionate. When our tongues met, the metal stud didn't bother me in the least. I marveled at Ted's skills as a male prostitute. Doing sex work in a bathhouse is more demanding than in any other setting. Periodically, the pace in a bathhouse can be hectic, since all potential clients are congregated in the same place and ready for instant action. The worker does not have time to psyche himself up between clients.

When we were done, I showed him a copy of *A Consumer's Guide*. He leafed through the book for a moment, then asked, "Do you mind if I come back with my lover? He will be interested in your book. He hustles here, too."

"Tell me about him."

"He's a black guy from Boston."

"Why didn't you mention this earlier? I told you that I liked darker people."

He smiled mischievously. "On the job, we're competitors."

He left the room. A few minutes later he came back with his lover in tow. "This is my partner, Jamil," he told me. Jamil was some ten years Ted's senior and much more my type. As he shook my hand he said, "Hi, my name is Jamil. In real life, I'm a poet."

"Working in the bathhouse is your hobby?"

"I wish. It brings in enough money for Ted and me to survive. When I have the time, I do my poetry."

The three of us chatted for a while. First we talked about my book, then about their experiences in the bathhouse. A group of voyeurs congregated in front of my cubicle, expecting to see us in action. I closed the door, but with three persons in the tiny cubicle, it quickly grew too hot. As soon as I reopened the door, a bunch of new voyeurs took up their positions.

When Ted and Jamil finally left, I rested for a while. As is customary in bathhouses, I left my door open. Noncharging visitors would be welcome.

A man walked into the cubicle. Brazenly, he sat down on the bed and started touching me. Law number one of gay bathhouses is that once you score, you will score again and again. It's just the first time that can be so damned hard.

My visitor was a man in his forties, an East Indian born in Trinidad. His name was Narayan. Although not terribly attracted to him, I didn't mind him in my cubicle, playing with my body. "Frankly, Narayan," I said to him, "I just had someone in the room. I'm not in shape to do it again. But you're welcome to stay." I probably was in shape, but it would have had to be a cuter man than Narayan to bring out my full potential.

"I know you had someone, actually two guys, here."

"You were watching?"

"Everybody was."

"Well, unfortunately, we didn't give a good show. We were just talking."

"They were two hustlers, yes?"

"If you say so."

"This place is *crawling* with them," he said with great disdain.

"Don't knock it. Who knows whether I would have met anyone had it not been for Ted—I mean, the fairer one."

"Sure you would."

"How do you know this?"

"You would compromise your standards."

I thought about his assertion for a moment. "You're right. This has happened to me many times in the past. I had to lower my standards in bathhouses. I didn't like it, though."

I could understand Narayan's resentment. For the average Torontonian, hiring a hustler in the bathhouse would have made for an expensive evening. To the sex worker's fee, one had to add the admission to the bath. My case was different. The exchange rate between the Canadian and U.S. dollar favored the latter; I was used to paying for sex workers' services; and I was on vacation.

"Do you know that sometimes the guys that hustle here give it away for free?" Narayan asked.

"No. But it's their own body. They can sell it or give it for free."

"They're unfair competition."

I could have marshaled a lot of arguments to refute his statement, but they would all have been hurtful. I decided not to answer. But in my mind things were pretty clear: If I had to choose between Ted and Narayan, I would have opted for Ted in spite of his fee. Had Ted been an ordinary patron and not a sex worker, he would have been choosy about his sex partners. He probably would have rejected Narayan and me. Had there been no sex workers at this bathhouse, I and many other patrons wouldn't have been there in the first place.

We chatted for a while and then I decided to call it an evening. I took a shower and made a final round. Jamil and Ted must have been with clients. A third sex worker, a Peruvian guy, was on duty. By my standards, he was more attractive than his two colleagues. (Three nights later, I engaged his services.) Absolutely nobody else in whom I was interested was in the bathhouse. Two patrons were standing ahead of me in the check-out line. Both complained to the attendant about the hustlers. When it was my turn, I said to him, "I'm glad that you allow hustlers at this bath. How do most customers feel about it?"

"Half and half," he said. "Some people come here for the prostitutes. A lot of queens are just jealous that other people are having a good time. And, you know, lots of gay men hate hustlers."

Chapter 4

The New Professionalism—
Does It Benefit Clients?

I believe that, in *A Consumer's Guide to Male Hustlers,* I portrayed sex workers in a positive light. The overall purpose of that book was to encourage readers to consider the use of their services in a safe and effective manner. I wrote it from the point of view of a consumer, rather than to endear myself to sex workers. Understandably, while most workers I spoke to were satisfied with my book, they objected vehemently to my statement that "With the notable exception of masseurs, [escorts'] financial expectations are off the wall" (p. 60).

The new professionalism has helped raise workers' financial expectations even more steeply. The question, from the clients' perspective, is whether sex workers' new professionalism benefits *them.*

Let's explore what professionalism means in this context. Before professionalism, when hustlers were invariably picked up in public places, johns got their tricks "as is." Some hustlers needed to take a shower; others were not internally clean enough for penetration; frequently, some were desperately hungry and had to be fed so that they could concentrate on the job. The majority of street hustlers failed to show up for future appointments. The fees these guys charged depended not only on what the market dictated but on their financial situation at a given moment (pp. 57-59).

Like postmodern sex workers, nonprofessional hustlers also negotiated the length of the session. It was usually "for a bit" or "overnight." Because the johns usually provided the transportation to and from the meeting place, the session length could not be calculated as precisely as it is today. The new professional escorts, especially ones working for agencies, start their chronometers upon arrival. The session is over in precisely sixty minutes (or, optionally, additional hourly fees may be added). In an article on the Web, "Escort Etiquette," an Australian sex worker writes: "Remember that it is not just the escort's responsibility to keep an eye on the time. If you agreed upon one hour, then remember that it is from the time he arrived, not the time you go to bed."[1]

Some professionals get so carried away with the value of their time that they even outdo lawyers with their "billable hours." For instance, some escorts will charge their *regular* clients a per-hour fee for being wined and dined or taken out to a show. Their rationale is that they lose potential income by spending their time with clients who treat them. After all, escorts get paid for escorting. Do they get many takers? You bet!

Some sex workers have already come up with a linguistic handle for such practices. Like mental health workers, they have started to "observe boundaries." They must not fraternize with their clients unless they are paid for it. The new professionalism frowns upon any nonmonetary interaction above and beyond the sex act. This limited job description is not what I desire. For me, sex with an escort is not only to get off. It is also to form an affectionate human bond. Luckily, less-than-professional sex workers and I cross boundaries all the time.

* * *

In the last chapter of *A Consumer's Guide,* I portrayed Michael, my regular sex worker as of 1998. At the beginning of the new millennium, Michael is still a regular. At this writing, he has been my steady for over three and a half years. In April 2000, I celebrated my fourth consecutive birthday in his sensuous embrace. Michael usually arrives at my place after a day's work. Sometimes, he will prepare himself a sandwich while I do other things. While he—or sometimes both of us—eat, we'll talk leisurely for an hour or so. We share with each other our achievements and frustrations since our last meeting, discuss a film one of us saw, or whatever. We *never* talk about sex to arouse each other, let alone watch pornography. I never touch Michael before we go into my dedicated sex room. (This is a boundary *I* observe with all my workers.) After he eats, Michael takes a shower. I have never known anyone who takes longer showers than

Michael. At long last, we'll start the sex session. When it is over, we rest in bed and talk some more—again, not about sex.

A professional worker would have taken a bath and eaten at home. The stopwatch would have been started as soon as he rang my doorbell. If I wanted to chat with him, it would be on my time. If he wanted to converse with me about his life or interests, I would feel that he was wasting my precious sixty minutes.

For the first year of our acquaintanceship, Michael was my only sex worker. Then he went to Los Angeles for a while and I had to find a substitute. This is how Winston Lee became my second worker. After Michael's return to San Francisco, I saw the two of them on a rotating basis. Winston will be portrayed in Chapter 11. For the moment suffice it to say that, while it lasted, Winston and I became closer emotionally than I had ever been with any sex worker.

From our second sex session onward, I helped Winston with his term papers (his English is shaky), and he was my computer troubleshooter. This was always done "as needed," never on a quid pro quo basis. Winston worked too many hours and sometimes didn't attend to his schoolwork until very late in the day. Occasionally, I had to stay up into the wee hours to receive his e-mailed term paper and return the copyedited version via e-mail. When my computer crashed, Winston came over as soon as possible, spending many hours to restore it.

Winston really was a perfect *virtual* boyfriend. Both of us got so much out of our interaction because the sex-for-money exchange, the time spent, and the extracurricular activities were all intertwined. It was *our* unique arrangement to meet *our* particular needs rather than a standardized, professional escort-client deal.

Michael observes plenty of boundaries of his own. For example, he pronounces various common words incorrectly: Suspicious comes out as "auspicious," regret becomes "fregret, and vagina is transformed into "fagina." Michael is aware that he has a speech impediment. Having been a teacher much of my life, I offered to help him with this problem. I didn't want him to appear stupid or uneducated. He resisted all my efforts to teach him anything. "But Michael," I told him more than once, "I used to teach foreign students English. I'm just as professional a teacher as you're an escort. Maybe even more so."

"I can't let you teach me."

"Why not?"

"Because I work for *you*."

"Well, pay me five dollars per lesson and I'll be working for *you*. Then you can fire me if you don't like the way I do my job."

But Michael has never allowed me to do speech therapy with him. After a while, I gave up on this idea because it caused tension between us. This is one of *his* boundaries.

I met Michael for the first time in March 1997. Michael's birthday was in November. Of course, I was ready with a monetary gift to celebrate the occasion. In addition, since Michael hardly ever goes out of town, I suggested that we drive somewhere to have lunch outside the city on his next day off. To my surprise, he rejected my offer and told me that sharing a pizza for supper on the day before his birthday, when we had a scheduled session, would be celebration enough. Over a period of time, I discovered that he had no interest whatsoever in being wined and dined by clients. Only well into our third year I finally understood his reluctance. Michael does not want to socialize with his clients on his own time.

Viewed logically, Michael's reluctance to go out with me does not make much sense. Usually he spends two and a half hours at my place. Add to it the time it takes me to drive him home at the end of the session, and it comes closer to three. Why would he begrudge a few more hours for an out-of-town excursion and lunch in a good restaurant?

Michael sees things differently. He does not wish to associate with his clients when he is off duty. Talking to me during our meetings is something that Michael considers part of the sex session. Actually, he even looks forward to it, because he, just like me, is a gabby person who enjoys chitchat. Another subtle fringe benefit comes of our conversations: Michael suffers from depression and takes prescribed medication for this condition. My tacit role has always been to lift *his* spirits. Still, I have learned to respect Michael's boundaries. They exclude social interaction with clients outside their homes.

In *A Consumer's Guide,* I point out that clients ought not to hog escorts' time. However much I like to gab, I am extremely sensitive to my regulars' time constraints. For instance, I had met Michael through his "model" ad in the *Bay Area Reporter.* His *nom de guerre* in the ad was Shawn. Within weeks of becoming my regular, Michael gave up the "Shawn" business. He didn't like escorting much, and liked even less the tremendous hassle of answering constant phone inquiries.[2]

Because of the physical stats (short and thin) in his ad, and his soft voice on the phone, many callers assume that he must be a bottom. Michael considers himself bisexual. Rarely, he will agree to be the top, but he is *never* a bottom. Most callers responding to his ad reject him when they learn to their surprise that he is unwilling to be topped. (As a sex worker, Michael has other attributes that appeal to certain clients: He is a great kisser, an accomplished cuddler, and kink and S/M friendly.)

Already handicapped by his limited sexual repertoire, Michael also lacks a large pool of potential clients. Physically, he is the opposite of "the boy next door." His skin is on the light end of black; he has a full head of dreadlocks dyed dark brown; he has never seen the inside of a gym; and at twenty-four years of age, he still looks boyish, even a tad androgynous.

Enough clients like me prefer Michael's appearance. With perseverance, he could have eked out a living from escorting. Once he started counting on me as a "regular," however, he was only too happy not to have to escort any longer. He does not escort *me*. When we get together for our sex sessions, we are (in his words) just "doing our little thing." I also do not consider him a sex worker. He is just my Michael who comes to see me once or twice a week.

When Michael absolutely must make more money than he takes in from his full-time job and from me, he resurrects Shawn for a few weeks by placing an ad. At first, he was embarrassed to answer his pager while at my place. I encouraged him to return calls except when we were in bed. Most of his pages are duds because he does not wish to be a bottom or because he is instinctively "auspicious" of the caller. On the rare occasions when Michael manages to set up a date, all our activities, except the length of his shower, are drastically abbreviated to accommodate the evening's second client. I drive him to his next appointment.

Doesn't the fact that I drive *my* Michael, who has just kissed my lips sweetly and sucked my cock skillfully, to his assignation *spoil the illusion?* What illusion—that between him and me there is more than just sex for money?

Not really. For starters, I am a graduate of the bathhouses. I, like everybody else there, have always tried to gain admission to as many cubicles as possible. I have been just as amorous with the occupant of room #123 as with the man at my next stop in room #321. Nowadays, I also have occasional free sex with "dirty young men"[3] who cheat on their wives or girlfriends to cavort furtively with a senior citizen. *Me, worry about Michael sowing his wild oats in another man's field?* All that matters is that the illusion be firmly in place while he is with me. In my hearts of hearts, I believe that more exists between us than just sex.

What, then, is the difference between Michael's boundaries of not allowing me to correct his speech or not wanting to be invited by me for a meal at a restaurant and the boundaries imposed on sex workers by their new code of professionalism?

My relationship with the vast majority of sex workers has always been unique. The way I interact with sex worker A is entirely different from my dealings with B; with C, I am confronted by a new challenge because I have never met someone like him before. However many sex workers I have been with, all are not just a blur in my mind.

In *A Consumer's Guide* I described at great length the special financial arrangements I have worked out with each of my regular sex workers. All of them have been nonprofessional by the current new standards. But suppose that money were not a consideration. Suppose I, too, could afford to hire (and would be attracted to) a top-of-the-line professional at $350 a shot? Would I engage him? Yes, I would, at least once, just so I would learn how affluent folks live. But knowing myself, I would revert to my nonprofessionals escorts and establish our special one-on-one relationships.

Chapter 5

Ass to Ass:
The Tantra Massage

In *A Consumer's Guide to Male Hustlers,* I discuss gay massages at great length.[1] Unlike sex workers, masseurs and masseuses have in place real, not imaginary, rules, conventions, codes of behavior, and boundaries. The vast majority of masseurs advertising in gay papers cross a major boundary by offering "release massages" or "full-body massages." In plain English, massages plus a hand job. *Professional* gay masseurs who adhere strictly to the rules do not make much of a living. Too much competition exists from masseurs advertising in the gay media who are willing to break rules and cross boundaries.

I know all of this from sad personal experience. In the 1980s, when I was still working as a hypnotherapist, it occurred to me to combine massage and hypnosis. I teamed up with handsome masseur, whom I found through his ad in a gay paper. To be completely professional, we rented a massage table. We advertised our services, offering a *nonsexual* massage-and-hypnosis session. The masseur's attractive face and muscular body adorned our large ad. We ran it for six weeks but received only one phone inquiry. Needless to say, the sole caller asked whether we would be willing to be a bit more flexible regarding our "nonsexual" policy. He wanted to be hypnotized, massaged, *and* released.

Professional masseurs use massage tables. Since such tables are adjustable, they allow the practitioner to position the client at an optimal angle. The table makes the massage more effective for the client and much easier on the practitioner. It also cuts down significantly on clients' hanky-panky during a release massage. The masseurs can reach any part of their clients' bodies, whereas the clients have much more restricted movement.

Most masseurs who advertise their services in the gay press do not bother with tables. First, tables are costly. Second, though usually portable, they are awkward to carry on out calls. Third, they often do not fit easily into clients' living quarters. Last but not least, unschooled practitioners, more numerous than certified massage therapists, find it physically difficult to give uninterrupted, hour-long massages. It becomes even more challenging if they have to give two or three massages in a row. Indulging the clients' hanky-panky on the bed is easier on them physically and more fun for the client. Once the sex play commences, clients tend to forget that the masseur has neglected certain parts of their bodies.

I am not a great fan of "release massages," because I like more than just a rubdown and a mechanical hand job. But these days I have been interviewing masseurs to fill Winston's position as one of my two regular sex workers. He is about to graduate with a BA degree and look for a full-time position while keeping his present part-time job. Pretty soon he won't have the time to see me.

In the sex workers' hierarchy, masseurs are relegated to the bottom rung. They are paid *less* for physically much *harder* work. Yet many practitioners who know pitifully little about their craft and whose only asset is their good looks feel more comfortable advertising their sexual services in the massage section. (Maddeningly, all too often the more *un*attractive the masseur the more professional his massage and vice versa.) I believe there are two reasons for this. First, technically speaking, "release" masseurs are not prostitutes—at least not in their own eyes. Second, it is completely up to them how far they will go with a given client. Contractually, they are only obliged to do the release thing. If they want to go beyond this point to please themselves or to earn more money, it is their call *after* seeing and evaluating the client. Sex workers do not have this luxury.

In the past, I have been able to work out satisfactory arrangements with nonprofessional masseurs. I made their work easier by dispensing with the massage altogether. They expanded their limits beyond the mechanical release to fulfill my sexual needs. The fee was affordable, because masseurs always charge less than escorts. Officially, they continued "massaging" me instead of doing sex work.

My sex workers and I usually have "soft sex"—that is, no penetration either way. Invariably, "hard sex" commands a higher fee. One of my sex workers, Étienne, with whom I came close to falling in love, told me that he considered our erotic sessions massage work. Occasionally, he asked me to screw him (see *A Consumer's Guide*, p. 134). But this happened only at the times he chose, not as part of our regular sessions.

The second masseur I tried out on my present search ran the following ad: "23 y/o Asian, 5' 10", 143, gives playful tantric and erotic full body massage in the nude, $40 out."

Tantra is associated these days with Tibet, but actually it originated in India. There is a lot more to this mystical teaching than sexual rituals, but this is what readily comes to mind when a masseur advertises a tantric massage. I knew before calling the masseur that the "Asian" in his ad meant East Indian. I have yet to meet a Tibetan sex worker, and other non-Indian Asians don't know or care about tantra. Suspiciously, his fee was $20 below the going rate. Often a bad reason is associated with a much lower-than-average fee. But I was curious about him; I had never had a tantric massage.

I called the number the masseur had listed in his ad. His lengthy outgoing message, referring callers to another number, was spoken in a unique accent. Tracing accents and speech patterns is a hobby of mine. I recognized the underlying Indian accent right away, but he also sounded like an English-speaking South African. I was mystified by this geographic jump. The speaker had a soft, soothing, seductive, somewhat high-pitched voice. I was intrigued.

When we finally made contact, he told me that his name was Sundaram. He pronounced his name in the staccato Indian cadence, not the mumbled English way. "Tell me about your massage, Sundaram," I said.

"Well, it's erotic and very sensual; tantric, you know. I make a lot of body contact, and I also do Thai massage. I do it in the nude, of course."

"What's a Thai massage?"

"I massage you with my feet as well as my hands." I had heard of such a technique practiced somewhere in the Far East but didn't remember whether it was in Thailand. I knew that the worst faux pas in Thai culture was to point one's foot at another person. How could this be reconciled with a foot massage? But I didn't want to quibble over the phone.

"Well, sure. I would like to try the foot massage."

"I charge forty dollars for forty minutes," Sundaram paused momentarily, then added rapidly, "and sixty dollars for a whole hour."

The leitmotif of A Consumer's Guide is that hustlers are independent contractors, managing their own businesses. Sundaram wrote his ad more like a shrewd businessman than a professional masseur. He would get more calls by quoting a lower-than-average fee and, once the caller was interested, negotiate a higher price. It was almost a bait-and-switch ad.

"I'll take the full hour. Where are you from, Sundaram?" I asked.

"I was born in Fiji. Ethnically, I'm an East Indian. My family moved from Fiji to Cape Town when I was a teenager."

Bull's-eye, I thought to myself. I had pegged him correctly. I had an instinctive feeling that Sundaram would not become one my regular sex workers. But I also sensed that his massage would be exciting. He told me that he was free that evening. At this point in the negotiations, the moment came to give him my address and directions to my place. This meant that I was committing my evening to him. If he didn't show up, for whatever reason, I couldn't summon the next suitable masseur. Masseur number one might be ninety minutes late (not an unheard of event), and run smack into number two. But that was a risk I had to take. We agreed on a 6:15 appointment. He promised that he would call when he was ready to leave.

He phoned at six to let me know that he was on his way, then, no Sundaram. I used to go through this kind of thing with new sex workers. But for over three years I have seen mostly my two regulars. Michael is punctual to a fault. When the bus is behind schedule (often enough in San Francisco!), he will call me from a pay phone. Winston, much busier than Michael, tends to run late, but uses his cell phone to let me know his new estimated arrival time.

At seven I dialed Sundaram's number, but there was only an outgoing message. Ten minutes later, the doorbell rang. I opened the door and ushered in my masseur for the evening. He shook my hand and took off his shoes before entering the house. He was out of breath but immediately started a long recitation about his automobile problems. "I'm sorry I'm late. My car stalled twice on my way here. And then I didn't dare drive my jalopy up your steep hill. I parked it before turning onto your street. Your hill is quite something."

"OK, don't worry. Sit down for a while. Make yourself comfortable," I said.

Sundaram reminded me of the hippies of yore. Under a nondescript kerchief, his thick black hair was long and unkempt. He wore a frilly unisex shirt and green pants. Around his neck hung three health-restoring semiprecious stones. The green one I recognized as a malachite. The red and turquoise stones I couldn't identify. Sundaram had regular East Indian features and was not bad looking. He smiled easily, displaying a strong bite marred by a few missing teeth. His large brown eyes sparkled. He spoke excitedly, in a bubbly fashion.

While we were undressing in the "trickery"—that's what I call my dedicated sex room—Sundaram told me that when not working as a masseur, he was a professional flutist and a singer. He was impressed when I told him that the trickery had once housed Jacinto, a fellow masseur, who plied his trade from there (see *A Consumer's Guide,* p. 60).

"Shall we start?" he asked, when we were both nude.

"*Acha hai,*" I answered. In Hindi, one of India's many official languages, this means "OK" and is used as often as its English counterpart.

"You speak Hindi?" He seemed surprised.

"I only fake it. I went to India to study yoga many years ago. I took up some Hindi before going to there. Which Indian language do you speak?"

"Gujarati. But I also understand Hindi."

As I had expected, Sundaram must have been some five years older than his advertised age of twenty-three. He had a neat, trim body, slightly hairy. I was pleasantly surprised that he was circumcised. I prefer cut cocks but had not expected this, given his ethnicity. In India, Moslems are always circumcised, as dictated by their religion, but Hindus are usually uncircumcised. (I knew that Sundaram was not a Moslem by his name. Moslems invariably have Arabic names. Sundaram hearkens back to Sanskrit.) "How come you cock is cut?" I asked.

"I had it done in San Francisco a few years ago. It's neater this way, don't you think?"

"Most definitely," I said. On principle, I really don't approve of circumcision, but I like my partners cut.

To massage a client's back effectively, the masseur must position himself well above the subject, for which the massage table is designed. When the masseur is in bed with the client there are a few ways this can be performed. All but one are physically difficult for the practitioner. The most convenient position is for the masseur to sit on the small of the client's back, straddling his body. For the latter, this is an erotic dream position.

Here is where we separate the professionals from the amateurs. The more professional the masseurs, the less likely they are to straddle their clients' bodies, even though it would make their job easier and more efficient. Masseurs who know little about massage codes of behavior use their common sense and instinctively position themselves on their clients' backs. The in-between group, the nonprofessionals who know a bit about massage work, are sometimes afraid of the great intimacy that is automatically established when they sit on clients' backs. They often need encouragement from their clients before assuming this position.

Sundaram sat on my back with great abandonment, making sure that I would feel not only his spread cheeks but also his dick. He started massaging my back forcefully. Massage is a combination of acquired skills and intuitive touch. Sundaram had more of the latter than the former. Actually, he did have the skills, but not the necessary book learning, that is, the physiological part. He didn't know, for instance, that the neck must not be massaged as vigorously as the back. But he did constantly ask for feedback from me, so no harm was done.

Suddenly, he stood on the bed and started working on my back with one of his feet. This resulted in a much more powerful massage. I enjoyed the new sensation, though sometimes I felt I was being stomped on and had to ask Sundaram to step more carefully. While doing his footwork, Sundaram told me that as soon as he had the money, he would travel to Thailand to learn more about massage.

Then he positioned himself on top of me, back to back. With his ass, he started massaging mine. He had put a lot of lotion on my backside earlier. My ass lubricated his, eliminating any friction between the two fleshy masses. Ass swiftly gliding on ass—I'd never experienced this kind of massage before. It wasn't really meant to improve my blood circulation or any of the other benefits ascribed to massage therapy. It did what it was supposed to do—heighten my sexual arousal. The maneuver impressed me so much that I closed my eyes, savoring the new sensation. I wish I had kept my eyes open and watched Sundaram's acrobatic feat in the large mirror mounted on one of the trickery's walls. I still wonder how he managed to perform this nifty "massage."

Once the masseur asks the client to lie face up, we again separate the professionals from the amateurs. The professional and semiprofessional masseurs will massage a client's entire body and only then turn their attention to the cock. By then the hour is almost over, and the practitioner a bit weary. Reluctantly and mechanically, the masseur performs the obligatory masturbatory manipulations. His apathy communicates itself to the client, who will often oblige and finish the job on his own. In the end, the client knows better than the masseur how to bring himself to the climax.

Nonprofessionals, when faced by a client's erect cock, finally find themselves on *terra cognita*. Sometimes they'll neglect the arms, the hands, and the feet altogether. They will massage the chest perfunctorily and then concentrate on the cock. Clients tend to overlook such lapses because cock massage is so much more fun. Depending on the masseur's imagination, the client's testicles and anus may be incorporated into the climax massage. The masseur has ample time to be playful. So much time, in fact, that with fast climaxers the massage can be over in less than an hour.

As Sundaram was manipulating my cock he started humming to himself. Knowing that he was a vocalist, I asked, "Will you sing for me, please?"

"Do you want me to?"

"Yes, very much."

"I can sing in Gujarati. I also know Brazilian songs. Which do you prefer?"

"Both."

Softly, in a high tenor voice, he started his songs. I am not a good judge of singing, but I enjoyed the performance. Never before had I been masturbated and sung to at the same time. I drew Sundaram's body closer to mine and was "released" to the sound of a Gujarati love song. *"Acha hai!"* I exclaimed as soon as I caught my breath.

At some point during the evening, I told Sundaram how the trickery came into being. It had been carved out of the kitchen to construct a small massage room for Jacinto, my former housemate.

While we dressed, Sundaram asked, "Do you know much about buying massage tables?"

"Why?"

"They're so expensive."

"Yes, I do." Jacinto had purchased a massage table as soon as he moved out of my place to live with his new lover. Both he and his lover wanted to decrease the physical intimacy between Jacinto and his clients. "Why are you interested in a table?" I asked Sundaram.

"Well, if I had one it would make me more professional."

"Sundaram, if you perform your massage on a table you or your client or both will fall off and get seriously hurt. Your massage is fine. It's great fun. It's unique. Learn more about Thai massage, if you can afford it. But don't become a massage-table professional."

"Well, I, too, was thinking about this. Maybe I can buy a thick futon and have the customers lie on the floor."

"Some will do that, but others will resist lying on the floor. Leave well enough alone. Do it on the client's bed. You're a wonderful masseur." I gave him a big hug.

Chapter 6

Sex-Plus Relationships

I wrote *A Consumer's Guide to Male Hustlers* as a how-to book. I wanted to tell readers all they needed to know about hiring and interacting with their sex workers on a win/win basis. The purpose of *this* book is to introduce the possibility of having a special relationship between clients and their workers. This is a much loftier goal; it cannot be taught in ten easy steps. Nor can it be expected that every encounter with a sex worker will end in a special relationship. If, after finishing this book, readers would be open-minded enough to allow for the eventuality of creating more than just sex-for-money relationships with their workers, I will have achieved my objective.

By "special relationship" I mean that between client and sex worker an exchange of money for sex *and more* occurs. The "more" can be a common intellectual pursuit, a spiritual practice, shared social activities, and even profound sexual interaction beyond what the agreement calls for.

In the following chapters I will sketch portraits of six workers, past and present, with whom I have had sex-plus relationships. In some cases, the "sex-plus" eventually grew into an abiding nonsexual friendship. Each special relationship with individual workers has been completely different; they themselves have been dissimilar from each other. But with each of them I established a sex-plus relationship.

Describing a yearned-for outcome of hustler/client interaction, Dr. John De Cecco writes: "[T]he client . . . hopes that the hustler will fall in love with him—that their crass business relationship will be metamorphosed into high romance."[1] In *A Consumer's Guide to Male Hustlers* (p. 98), I point out that attempting to make the sex worker into a lover is almost always doomed to fail. Yet I have achieved the sex-plus relationship time and time again with my own workers.

Many sex workers as well as their clients will tell you that a straightforward exchange is good enough for them. Ideally, the client gets good sex and rewards the worker generously. This quid pro quo is, after all, what happens in other professional exchanges. But because of the physical and sometimes even emotional intimacy with sex workers, there can be more than a sex-for-money transaction. I will give examples of sterile sex worker/client interactions, as well as sex-plus relationships between the two parties.

Omar, whom I have already mentioned, and who will be featured in a later chapter, is a former sex worker of mine. Now we are just good friends and get together socially on a regular basis. One afternoon he called me and said that he would be thirty-five minutes late because John, a regular client, had just requested an instant session. Omar, a punctual person, arrived exactly thirty-five minutes later. "How did you calculate precisely the time it would take you to get here?" I asked him.

"Simple. It takes me fifteen minutes to drive to John's house. I park in his driveway. Another fifteen minutes to turn the trick, and then five minutes to get to your place."

"But how can you predict exactly how long John will keep you?"

"I have been with him half a dozen times. It's always the same scene. When I arrive he asks 'Is your dick hot today?' I reply, 'As soon as you take it in your mouth, it'll be hot and hard and ready to shoot.' We stand in the living room. He takes off his clothes but doesn't want me to undress. I squeeze his nipples real hard for a few minutes, then he goes down on his knees. I unzip my fly. I just stand there while he sucks me off. When I finish—you know it doesn't take me long—he says, 'Your cum tastes sweet today.' I say, 'Next time it'll taste sweeter.' As he puts on his clothes, he asks, 'Is your dick still hot?' I reply, 'It's always hot with you around me.' When he's dressed, he gives me my one hundred dollars, and I'm out of there. Fifteen minutes is all it takes. I timed it."

"What sort of a guy is John?"

"He's a fat man in his forties. Otherwise, he's not bad-looking. Has a nice house, expensive furniture. Probably makes a bundle. Likes classical music a lot. That's all I know about him."

"Have you told him that you're a guitarist? What *does* he know about you?"

"Just that I have a hot dick."

"Who came up with that 'hot dick' baby talk?"

Omar reflected for a moment. "You know, I'm not sure. I think he scripted our sex sessions this way. Whatever the reason, the way we do it, it's over in a jiffy. That's all that matters to me."

"If he asked you, would you stay longer?"

"I suppose so. Isn't it usually one hour? But he never asks me to stay after he gets off."

"Do you know why?"

"No. And I don't care. The faster the better."

Michael, my regular, tells me similar stories about his clients. He calls one of his regulars "What's-his-name." I am sure that Michael knows the client's real name, and this is just a put-down. "When I get there, What's-his-name says, 'Good to see you, Lon.'"

"I thought your escort name is Shawn."

"It is Shawn. He forgot."

"Why don't you correct him?"

"What for? Lon, Shawn, it's all the same to me. There's always some boring porn on the TV. He plays the VCR too loud. Maybe he's a little deaf. He puts an envelope on the table with my money. He asks me if I want a beer. I say 'OK.' He brings in two beers. We drink and watch the stupid video. I take two or three sips. Then he grabs the bottles and says, 'Let's get started, Lon.' Why don't he let me finish my drink? I ain't the one rushin' him. I follow him to the bedroom. He likes to undress me. He licks my body all the time. He drools over me. I don't like that. Then he pulls me on the bed, cuddles with me, and licks my body and balls some more. Then we sixty-nine for a few minutes, and then he comes."

"You let him come in your mouth?" I was surprised. Michael is the most health-conscious escort I have ever met. He used to do AIDS outreach work at the bathhouses in New York City.

"Of course not. He had an operation and can't come. He says he comes inside hisself. In the beginning, I was auspicious of him. Then I saw for myself that when he came he was totally dry. What's the operation called?"

"Prostate surgery."

"Yeah, *prostrate.*"

"When you're done, does he ever talk to you?"

"No, he gives me the envelope with my money. He just don't like to talk much."

* * *

In the 1970s, as the Vietnam War was winding down, there were many Vietnamese male hustlers around. I know nothing about their female counterparts. All the Vietnamese male sex workers I have been with (right into the new millennium) have done their sex work to augment their income, not because of dire poverty.

Patrick was one such Vietnamese. I had first met him through an escort agency. After that, we made an arrangement to see each other bypassing the agency and its referral fees. I had mixed feelings about doing this. In the end, though, it turned out for the best. Soon the agency went out of business. Had I kept booking Patrick through them, I would have been unable to contact him on my own.

The first time I met Patrick, he told me that he was a student at UC Berkeley in his junior year. "What are you majoring in?" I asked.

"Spanish."

It was odd that this guy who had learned English only in his early teens would take up Spanish as his major. Since I wanted to practice my Spanish, I started speaking it with him. He had remarkably good pronunciation and a large vocabulary. After more than an hour of prattling in Spanish, I remembered that Patrick was with me for more than language practice. He turned out to be a good partner in bed, and for close to a year he was one of my regulars.

Both of us were genuinely interested in practicing Spanish. This common interest gave rise to a routine. Patrick would arrive around six p.m. I would have a pizza ready for both of us. While having a leisurely supper, we would converse in Spanish. Then we would have sex. Both of us took our Spanish practice seriously. I kept the dictionary on the floor, near the bed, in case we needed to look up a word.

Many years later I learned that putting on a happy face is mandatory in Vietnamese culture. I did not know that Patrick was ill at ease with his sex work. He did tell me at some point that he was seeing only me, but I assumed this was because of his schoolwork. One day, after the pizza, he said to me in English, "Joseph, today will be our last time."

"Why, Patrick?"

"I want to start *dating* men again. I've never felt comfortable doing this. It'll be impossible for me to date and do *this*."

"That's too bad, Patrick. I really enjoy our sessions. I'll miss the Spanish and even more the . . . other thing. Can I ask you for a favor? My birthday is next week. I planned on being with you that day. Could you postpone your retirement by one week?"[2]

"Of course, Joseph."

Patrick arrived the next week with a small painting as my birthday gift. I still have it.

Obviously, clients cannot just engage a sex worker and expect that they will share a common interest, as I did with Patrick. But they can be open to something of this sort. I was open to it by asking Patrick what his major was. Had I not asked this one question, we never would have developed our "Spanish connection."

By being willing to talk, I have learned a lot from my sex workers, probably more than from my free sexual encounters. Men I meet socially often converse about subjects with which I have some familiarity, such as current events, movies, the stock market, and literature. My sex workers, especially the ones I have picked up on the streets, have taught me things which ordinarily I would never have learned. For instance, due to Étienne, the subject of Chapter 11 in *A Consumer's Guide,* I learned a great deal about hip-hop dancing. I can see Rick Whitaker of *Assuming the Position* wrinkling his nose. My answer to Rick would be, "OK, Rick, ballet is *real* art. Hip-hop street dancing is . . . whatever it is. But, still, I'm a more well-rounded person for knowing something about hip-hop."

* * *

One evening, late in the 1970s wandering along Market Street near Castro, I casually cruised a waiflike guy. He had a winsome air about him. What attracted me most was his ethnic mix. He looked Asian, though to my trained eye it was impossible to pin down which part of the continent his folks hailed. In spite of the cold weather, he wore only a tank top and a pair of pants. His light-brown skin was completely hairless. Noticing that I was interested in him, he said to me, "My name is Terry. I need twenty-three dollars to take the bus to Fullerton. If you can give it to me, I'm yours for one hour."

"When does the hour start?"

"When we get to your place."

"How old are you?"

"I just turned twenty in August. I'm a Leo. You know what that means, don't you?"

"Of course." Actually, I had no idea.

I had not intended to pick up a hustler on that particular evening. But I liked Terry's bold, no-nonsense approach. He had an air of purposefulness about him. I was pretty sure that he would be as focused in bed as he was single-minded about his bus ticket to Fullerton. "OK, Terry, let's go."

While I was driving to my home, Terry said, "This has been a terrible evening for me. I myself am a powerful witch, but the two other witches I tackled were even more skillful than me."

Some men would have ordered Terry out of their vehicle right then and there, because the mention of witches would have spooked them. Others would have kicked him out for being too strange. *I* wanted to get to know him better. Unfortunately, at that point in time, the only witches I was familiar with were the "three weird sisters" in Shakespeare's *Macbeth*.

"Terry, you're a man, so you must be a warlock, not a witch." He was a man for sure, though not too manly a man.

"No, I am a *witch*. Both men and women are called witches." Then I remembered that the three weird sisters wore beards,[3] making them . . . transgender witches?

"Do you know much about wicca? That's the correct name for our craft."

"Nothing at all, Terry."

Terry was a native of Hawaii—a Japanese-Filipino ethnic blend. He was attending community college near Fullerton but took little interest in his studies. However, he struck me as a fairly intelligent young man.

Had Terry had his way with me that night, he would have topped me. His outwardly androgynous appearance belied what he enjoyed doing most in bed. "I told you that I was a Leo," he said petulantly when I refused his offer to screw me. "I dominate!"

In the end, it turned out to be a fun evening for both of us. Terry got his twenty-three dollars to return to Fullerton, where he lived with his parents, and I had my first lesson in wicca.

Over the next eleven years, I saw Terry at irregular intervals. Through him I got a thorough education in wicca, the witchcraft (some say paganism) practiced by the Anglo-Saxons before the advent of Christianity. By the time I met Étienne (see *A Consumer's Guide,* Chapter 11), I knew enough about "rituals" to hold my own when he talked about this subject. (Étienne's rituals were modified Haitian, not Anglo-Saxon, but the sum and substance of the ceremony was the same.) Far from sorcery, I regarded Terry's and Étienne's rituals as harmless, self-empowering tools.

A few years after meeting Terry, I started conducting self-hypnosis workshops at the College of Marin. I always taught at least one session on visualization techniques as an adjunct to self-hypnosis. "When one performs a ritual in wicca, the traditional Anglo-Saxon witchcraft, one is, in fact, doing a visualization," I told my students. I discussed briefly how the ritual enhanced the visualization.

During the break, a matronly student came up to me and said, "You surprised me with your comments about wicca."

My heart sank. I was teaching in Marin County, the heartland of New Age. Still, witchcraft is offensive to many people. Had I broached a taboo subject? "How did I surprise you?" I asked her.

"You don't look or dress like a person who would know much about wicca," my student said. I took this as an enormous compliment. Months later, when I saw Terry, I thanked him for having expanded my horizons.

As for Terry, in 1989 I engaged his services to help me set up my first computer. He had evolved from a powerful witch into an equally powerful, self-taught computer expert.

* * *

In Chapter 2, I discussed my aborted meeting with sex worker Oscar on the occasion of my sixty-fifth birthday. By that time I had known Oscar for close to eight years. He is African-Panamanian on his father's side, and African American on his mother's, born and bred in San Jose, California. His skin is very dark, but his coarse, straight black hair comes from a different gene pool. I have always considered him somewhat ugly because he is cross-eyed and has bad teeth. That said, I have always been tremendously aroused by him— and he by me.

From our first meeting, there has always been sexual and emotional tension between us. Oscar has a high-pitched voice and speaks much too fast. When he gets excited, which is often, his voice becomes shrill, verging on hysterical. He is a bright guy. With little formal schooling under his belt, he is an avid reader and has a musical ear. He was raised by his mother and grandmother. All he ever got from his father was a Spanish surname.

A year after I met Oscar, I picked up a Hispanic guy on Polk Street. He turned out to be Oscar's long-term boyfriend.[4] Like Oscar, he was in his early twenties. I then knew for sure that I wasn't remotely Oscar's physical type. Nonetheless, my sex sessions with Oscar were not only technically accomplished but had another dimension—possibly a physical longing on Oscar's part for intimate contact with an older mentor. This longing communicated itself to me. Our sessions had a passion above and beyond good sex between client and worker. Sometimes, in the middle of a session, Oscar would complain that I never praised him. In my mind, I had a ready retort. "To be praised, you first must be praiseworthy." Of course, I didn't tell him this.

It was difficult to praise Oscar. Invariably, he managed to screw up things. From day one I considered him "bad news." But our intense sexual bond brought us back together time and again against my better judgment. Oscar was the only hustler who has ever threatened me with physical harm. (This was over my refusal to make a false statement on his behalf to his social worker. The threat was "I'll have to hurt you.") I wasn't too worried about it, but I also didn't dismiss it as mere bluster.

After Oscar threatened me, I avoided him. I did not see him for many months. One afternoon I was walking to my car, parked on Polk Street. I passed an unshaven, bedraggled, apparently homeless black man. Suddenly, the guy opened his arms and embraced me. "Don't you recognize me, Joseph?" he asked while hugging me.

Oscar's high-pitched voice was unforgettable. Still in shock, I was just about to ask, "Oscar, is that you?" Before I got the chance, he was kissing me on the lips, as he had always done. Immediately, my dick hardened. I could feel Oscar's stiffness through his pants.

I wish someone had taken photos of us at that moment. The embrace and kiss would have dispelled all sorts of stereotypes. The photos would have portrayed loving friendship between youthful and aging gays, homeless and homeowner, black and white.

Just as I had felt Oscar's stiffness, he must have sensed my sexual arousal. It would have been hypocritical to bid him a good day and move on. "Oscar," I asked, "what happened to you? You look a mess." No sooner did I say this than I realized that, once again, I was criticizing Oscar instead of praising him.

"This is how I look when I'm depressed."

It turned out that Oscar had a lot to be depressed about: unpaid rent, trouble with the law for soliciting, and a "contract" to hurt him put out by a street rival. When he asked me, "Can we start dating again?" my sexual attraction—and his looking up to me in spite of being resentful of me, overpowered my decision never to see him again.

"If you shave and clean up we can make a date for tomorrow."

* * *

If I am so successful with sex workers I pick up, and if they are sometimes even attracted to me physically, why don't I make them into my lovers? In Oscar's case the answer is straightforward. He was too much to take on as a lover. As a matter of fact, he was even too much as a hustler, but we had this crazy sexual bond. What about Patrick, then? He didn't care for me physically. We had an intellectual affinity, which made our sexual encounters more meaningful for both of us. But I wasn't boyfriend material for him.

Then what about all my other successful sex worker relationships? As the six following chapters will demonstrate, each relationship was in the sex-plus category. They were my sex workers; I was their client; but there was more to it for both parties. However, this does not mean that they coveted me for a boyfriend, nor that they would have made suitable lovers for me.

So, in the end, is it only about money? No. Just as for me it is sex-plus, for them it is money-plus. I can document this with a sad anecdote. In Chapter 8 I will sketch Beauregard, whom I knew from the age of nineteen until his death from AIDS some twelve years later. He had been my sex worker for only a year and a half. Then we became just friends. A week before he passed away, he wished to see one last time people who had played a significant role in his life. I was one of the visitors summoned to bid good-bye to my former sex worker, Beauregard.

Chapter 7

Playing Prisoner of War

Between 1973 and 1976 I didn't patronize any street hustlers. During this period I had a lover. We were far from monogamous—open relationships were in vogue—and had regular flings at the bathhouses. But it was not necessary or desirable for me to bring hustlers to *our* home.

During these three years, escort/model ads proliferated in the gay press. Although still with my lover, I read the ads avidly. I was struck by how much higher the escorts' fees were compared to those I paid street hustlers. When my lover and I ended our relationship, we chose to live together in the same rented house for a few months. Out of consideration for him, I didn't bring anyone home while he was there. For the first time, in the summer of 1976, I resorted to escorts advertising their services and operating out of their own homes.

Soon enough I understood why their fees were so much higher. They were not competing at all with the street hustlers. They were an entirely new class of sex workers. Nowadays, a number of ways exist to communicate with workers. In those prepager days, advertising workers had to have a private phone line. This was not horrendously expensive, but it was above and beyond what the majority of street hustlers could afford. To begin with, most of them were jobless. From such applicants, the phone company demanded a security deposit. In addition, they often had outstanding bills from their *previous* phone line, which had to be paid off before a new one could be installed. In any case, trying to get a phone installed often turned out to be an exercise in futility, because street hustlers moved a lot.

Many of the *new* escorts already had their own phones. All they needed to do was to insert an advertisement in a gay paper and, voilà, they were in business. Unlike their lowly street colleagues with their distasteful tasks, the escorts considered the new prostitution a challenge to be met head-on. *They* would never have stood on a street selling their bodies. But safely ensconced in their own apartments, or going to clients' homes by appointment, they felt venturesome. In the beginning, most of them did not depend exclusively on escort income to survive. Consequently, they were much more in control of their lives. In the worst-case scenario, if they could not stomach the client, they were in a position to abort the assignment without going hungry. In *A Consumer's Guide to Male Hustlers* (Chapter 6), I describe a night in the life of a Polk Street hustler eking out a living in San Francisco. At the beginning of his "shift" he hopes to take in $75. Many hours later, all he gets is a place to sleep and drugs in exchange for sexual services.[1] Such calamities did not befall the new escorts.

In time, some street hustlers caught on, especially after the advent of the beeper, and upgraded themselves to escorts. But in the 1970s, escorts were not at all comparable to hustlers. For instance, my first two regular escorts owned their own automobiles; street hustlers often didn't even have a permanent roof over their heads. Because escorts' phone numbers could be traced, they were much safer than the anonymous street hustlers. Doing an in call (going to an escort's home) was almost totally safe.[2]

During the three months my ex-lover and I lived in the same house, I made the acquaintance of two escorts and one street hustler whom I sometimes brought home in the early afternoons on my day off, when my ex was still at work. I wrote about one of the escorts, Alfonso, in *A Consumer's Guide.*[3] The street hustler, Beauregard, will get his own chapter later on. Here I'll describe my experiences with the second escort I met that summer.

* * *

One day in September 1976, after reading the escorts' columns, I called this advertiser:

> Cute 26 y/o, playful, totally versatile Asian 5' 7", 139, $30 in, $50 out, call Alex today.

Alex's out call fee was higher than most advertisers. His in call fee was average. It was seven in the evening when I placed my call. Alex sounded good over the phone. "When do you want to come over? It's going to be a very a busy evening for me."

"Actually, I am calling to make a date for tomorrow evening."

"Can you come tomorrow at 5:30?"

"Why, is this better for you?"

"I give a special rate to early customers, twenty-five dollars for an in call. Make sense?"

Yes, it made sense. Still, on the street, I could get a hustler for $15. At that point in my life, I was not in a good position to shell out a small fortune for escorts operating out of their homes. Alex's discount was welcome. "I'll be there by five-thirty," I said.

Alex lived close to the cruisy section of Polk Street, which even in those days presented a parking challenge. When he opened the door, I was struck more by his living room, which I could see from the hallway, than by him. Against two walls were huge aquariums full of goldfish. Two smaller aquariums, which I saw when I was inside the room, housed colorful tropical fishes. For a moment I thought that I had rung the wrong bell.

"Alex?"

"Yes. Nice to meet you. Come in, make yourself comfortable." He pointed to a chair by a dining table and said, "Please sit down. Was it difficult to find a parking space?"

"Very. Before six there's hardly any parking on the streets around your house."

"I know. But I get so busy later at night. And I don't get off work until five. There's only *one* of me, you know!" When Alex said this he sounded like a diva, bemoaning the constant performances she has to give to satisfy her insatiable audiences.

"It's quite a hobby you have," I said, pointing to the wall-to-wall aquariums.

"It's not a hobby. I import my fishies from Hong Kong and sell them to my customers all over the country."

"You're an escort *and* a goldfish merchant?"

"Also a bank teller. Because of my mother I have to keep a regular job. I can't tell her that I'm hustling, can I? I lose a lot of business because I'm not at home during the day."

Just then the phone rang. Alex spoke in Cantonese for a moment. Then he cupped the mouthpiece and, in an exasperated whisper, told me, "It's my mother."

I don't understand Cantonese, though I can distinguish it from Mandarin, but I was ready to bet that the few words he kept repeating irritably were the English equivalent of "Yes, mother," and "OK, mother." Finally, the conversation ended. "My mother bugs me. She is so nosy. All I'm trying to do is to make a living. Do you want a glass of wine?" he asked.

"No, thanks. A soft drink would be fine." I was impressed by my surroundings. I had tricked with hustlers in their run-down hotels many times. Alex's place was the opposite of run-down. It was nicely furnished, though cramped by the four aquariums. Neatly arranged on the table was a stack of envelopes addressed to "Lloyd Lim." Most were airmail envelopes. Realizing that I must have noticed his mail, Alex said, "My real name is Lloyd. I use Alex in my 'Asian' ad; in the other one I don't write 'Asian' and call myself Bill. You know, like a company with many divisions, Alex and Bill compete against each other. Make sense?"

"Which division makes out better?"

"The Alex Division. The rice queens are more devoted to me."

Guys like me who appreciate Asian partners are referred to as "rice queens." I don't like this expression much. In the days before political correctness, it was considered a generic term. "Are you from Hong Kong?"

"Yes, I come here when I'm twelve years old."

Lloyd loved to talk. He was an ordinary-looking guy, not really handsome, with long black hair that was the style in those days. The phone rang once again. He listened for a moment, then said in English, "Please hold on." He went to the kitchen and came back with a piece of cake. Covering the mouthpiece, he said, "This will take a while. It's a long-distance call. Have some cake. It's pretty good."

Listening to Lloyd's side of the conversation, I gathered that the call was about goldfish. Lloyd was prescribing a fish medication. Idly, I nibbled at the chocolate cake. This was not your ordinary piece of cake. Lloyd must have bought it at some fancy bakery. Finally, he got off the phone. "They have some sick fishies in Massachusetts. They are healthy when I ship them. I sell the fishies, so I don't want them to die, make sense? You know that. . . ." The phone rang again.

"Yes, this is Bill," Lloyd said. He listened for a moment then answered the caller, "Yes, I'm a bottom, and we can do S and M." The caller asked another question and Lloyd replied slowly and clearly, "Yes, I can be a master *and* a slave. I do both. Make sense?" It took another five minutes before he hung up the phone. He scheduled an appointment for 7:30. Unlike me, he would charge the caller his full fee. Turning to me, Lloyd said, "There is only *one* of me, you know."

"Alex, I mean Lloyd, can we get started, and will you please not answer the phone?"

"But my customers *need* me. I have to take their calls. I'm out of the house for most of the day. In the evening I have to take their calls. Make sense?"

"I won't be able to concentrate if the phone keeps ringing." Seeing that he was displeased, I asked, "Why don't you buy an answering machine? Last week I was with another escort who has one." At the time, answering machines were a novelty.

"I am getting one next month."

"Well, take the phone off the hook while we're in the bedroom. This way your callers will think you are so popular that they can't get through and they'll try even harder to get hold of you."

With the phone off the hook, we went into the bedroom. It too had an immense aquarium as long as an entire wall. Swimming content-edly in it were large goldfish rather than "goldfishies." Lloyd's bed was made of a wooden frame with drawers for storage. The mattress fit into a platform on top of the frame. Protruding from the frame were three large metal fasteners. I wondered what these were all about. When Lloyd took his clothes off, I marveled at his hairless body. Otherwise, Lloyd's face and body, as well as his cock, were unremarkable. Maybe "passable" would be a better expression. His right ass-cheek had a small tattoo of a sailboat. Cute!

Midway through a session of heavy kissing and mutual blowing, Lloyd asked, "Do you want to play Vietnam Prisoner of War?"

"I've never played this game. How does it work?"

"I show you. Close your eyes for a moment."

Before I knew it, my body was fastened tightly to the bed with three wide leather straps. I must not have seen the straps before because they were between the bed and the wall. I was not tied up. Rather, I was immobilized. It was my first time with Lloyd, and I should have experienced some fear, especially since we had not discussed S/M activities before the session. But I had full confidence in Lloyd. It helped that I was in *his* apartment. After all, it is an S/M adage that you're always safer playing in the other guy's place. I was rather intrigued by how quickly he managed to immobilize me. "I am going to blindfold you now," he said, even as he was doing it with a large blue handkerchief. "We call this sensory deprivation. It make the prisoner talk. Make sense?"

At this point I should have panicked. But I felt completely relaxed. Powerless now, a grim idea came to mind. If Lloyd killed me, would he cut up my body and feed it to his fishies? He sat on my belly and started gently squeezing my nipples. Then, gradually, he kept increasing the pressure. All the while, he told me a convoluted prisoner-of-war story.

Usually, I hate such fantasy talk because the narration is so poor. Surprisingly, I enjoyed Lloyd's presentation. He spoke English well, though he remained a captive of Cantonese grammar. In his English speech, as in his native language, only the present tense existed. Lloyd's timeless present tense served to enhance the reality of the game. There was no past and no future for me. There was just Lloyd, the sadistic camp commandant, torturing me, the powerless prisoner. Periodically he punctuated his interrogation with a menacing "I want more information," and pulled my hair or my ears. It was playful enough not to cause any real damage and real enough to introduce an element of apprehension.

Then Lloyd started biting my nipples really hard. I was just about to ask him to stop when he bent over me, thrust his tongue into my mouth, and force-kissed me. The pain in my nipples combined with his unexpected violent kissing brought me close to an orgasm. Intuitively, or maybe just from experience, Lloyd became aware that the countdown was close to zero. Letting go of my left nipple, he shifted his attention to my penis and brought me swiftly to an explosive climax.

I was still blindfolded when he started licking my lips with his tongue and said, "You're an excellent prisoner. Next time we play that I am your prisoner. Or maybe we play Chinese Torture of a Thousand Spanks. Then I shoot at the same time you come. Today I have to save my cum for the other customers." He removed my blindfold and undid the straps.

He rushed to the corridor. I heard him put the receiver back on the base. No sooner did he do this than the phone rang. Carrying the phone, which had a long cord attached to it, Lloyd returned to the bedroom and gave me a washcloth. He managed to talk to me, even as he conversed with the caller. Before I left his apartment he had booked one additional customer for the evening, and two for the next day.

As I was cleaning up, Lloyd entered the bathroom, drew a little water into the tub, and washed his crotch, preparing for his next customer. Rather than turn me off, his "whore's bath" titillated me. What he needed, I thought, was a European-style bidet. After dressing, I handed him his money. Unlike street hustlers, he put it away in his dresser without counting it. Momentarily, he wasn't answering any calls. "The most important thing for me is to be at home when a customer phone me. This is why I charge so much for out calls. If you become a regular I give you the same price any time of day. Make sense?"

"Well, thank you, Lloyd. I will become a regular. Where did you buy the delicious cake?"

"At noon today, I have lunch at the St. Francis Hotel. I buy extra dessert for my mom and for customers like you who have to wait when I'm on the phone."

"Lunch at the St. Francis? Aren't you a bank teller?"

"I am. My mother make me work there. I lose money when I am not at home. Make me mad. I treat myself to a good lunch at a nice place. Make sense?"

"All within one hour?"

"It's a big rush for me. I take taxis."

"Makes sense," I said as I left his apartment.

I felt great when I drove home from Lloyd's aquariums. The unexpected experience was quite intense. I wondered whether it could be duplicated in future encounters without the element of surprise. But Lloyd knew of so many other games we could play. Clearly, he was familiar with a great variety of sex roles and seemed to enjoy performing them all. Remarkably, he was also bent on expanding the horizons of his customers.

As I had foreseen, the rest of my sex sessions with Lloyd were never as intense as our first encounter. But they were fun enough and we grew fond of each other. We played many of Lloyd's games. He liked to change roles, sometimes twice within one session.

I came to regard Lloyd as a CEO managing three divisions of the same company. The "Alex Division," selling sex to the rice-queen market, competed against the "Bill Division," offering the same item to the general gay population. The "Lloyd Division" of the business sold goldfish throughout the country. A few months into our acquaintanceship, Lloyd resigned his teller's job to have more time for the customers of all three divisions. His mother certainly could not have blamed him for not making enough money.

I liked being one of Lloyd's customers. He provided excellent service with a smile and a piece of cake. But there was an even more intriguing aspect to Lloyd. When I was a schoolboy, I had read many of Pearl Buck's novels. They were all set in China at the beginning of the twentieth century. (She was awarded the Nobel prize for Literature in 1938.) I asked Lloyd whether he had read any of her works. He didn't even know Pearl Buck's name. Yet he spoke like a Chinese courtesan in one of Buck's novels. He repeated his two catchphrases, "There is only one of me," and "I want my customers to be devoted to me," at each of our sessions.

For close to four years I was one of Lloyd's regulars. We became so friendly that he asked me to take a present to his uncle when I visited Hong Kong in 1980.

In the early 1980s, I started seeing a different group of escorts and lost contact with Lloyd. Then, one day, I don't remember the year, I decided to call him. I wanted to see how he was and maybe even do an in call. Lloyd said, "Oh, I am so glad to hear from you, Joseph," Lloyd said. "What a nice surprise!" We chatted for a while, then I asked him, "Can we make a date?"

"I don't make dates any more. I sold my bed. I just have a small bed now."

"It's OK, Lloyd. With you, I don't mind doing it in a narrow bed."

"Not in this bed. It's too . . . no, Joseph, it's impossible." There was so much sadness in his voice when he said this. After I hung up I realized that a bad disease was decimating our community and Lloyd must have caught it.

There is no closure to this story. When I called Lloyd a few weeks later, his number had been disconnected. I never heard from him again. I didn't have his mother's phone number to find out what had happened to him. This was a harbinger of the same tale with other sex buddies of mine. One day they just disappeared, never to be heard from again.

Chapter 8

"I Used to Be Joseph's Little Prostitute"

All things being equal, I prefer picking up street sex workers. Face to face, it takes me but a second to know whether "chemistry" exists between us. When an escort arrives as a result of a phone or an Internet appointment, a mental adjustment almost always needs to be made. What the client visualized in his mind's eye when speaking to the sex worker on the phone does not conform to what he sees in front of him. This usually holds true even if the worker has a photo in the paper or on the Web.

But all things are not equal. Unfortunately, picking up sex workers in the streets is more dangerous than through ads. Still, it took me almost ten years to wean myself completely from street workers. In 1976, I was not yet ready to meet only advertising sex workers. It was not only related to the instant-chemistry issue. The guys listed under the banner of "Models and Escorts" in the gay press charged twice as much as street hustlers.

In those days, to the great chagrin of the management of the St. Francis Hotel, the hustler scene in San Francisco was concentrated on the south side of this establishment, where Geary and Powell Streets intersect.

I arrived there at 7:30 p.m., quite early for street workers to be out in force. One of the few workers on duty caught my attention immediately. He was not particularly handsome, especially because he suffered from a serious case of acne. What he had going for him was youthfulness and assertiveness. The moment our eyes locked, he asked, "Are you looking for a date?"

He had an engaging smile, though his teeth were crooked. I stopped in front of him. "Well, yes, I'm looking for a date. My lover—more correctly, my former lover—is out of town and I have the house all to myself."

"What sign are you?"

"What *sign?*"

"What's your zodiac sign?"

"I'm a Taurus."

"I'm a Virgo. We'll be compatible."

"Now that we know that we'll be compatible, what is your name? Mine is Joseph."

"Larry." He reflected for a moment, then said, "No, I trust you. I'll give you my real name, not the fake one I use for hustling. It's Beauregard."

In spite of his somewhat ordinary looks, the guy had a presence. "You're my first 'Beauregard.' I like your name. Do you go by 'Beau,' or do you prefer to be called by your full name?"

"I prefer Beauregard."

"How old are you, Beauregard?" I was reasonably sure that he was over eighteen but I wanted to hear it from him.

"I've just turned nineteen."

In short order we agreed on a fee of fifteen dollars and what we would do in bed. Intuitively, I was absolutely certain that Beauregard would make a good sex partner. I detected a Southern drawl in his speech. While I was driving, I asked, "Where are you from, Beauregard?"

"I was born in Louisiana, raised in South Carolina, and came here from San Diego."

"What did you do in San Diego?"

"I was in the Navy."

"And?" He was too young to be a veteran.

"I didn't want to play with the Navy guys anymore."

"Play?"

"Yeah, I told them I didn't like them anymore." He sounded like a petulant child. "That was three weeks after I joined the Navy."

"And they let you go?"

"No, they threw me in the brig. But I kept telling them that I didn't want to play with them no more. They made me see two psychologists and a psychiatrist. Finally, they gave me an administrative discharge and let me go. Then I came to San Francisco because I'm gay."

"When did you arrive here?"

"The day before yesterday. You're my second john. The second john not only in San Francisco but in my whole life."

"Don't worry. I'll be a very good john. How did you know where to hustle?"

"I asked a dude when I got off the bus in San Francisco."

"You mean, you just asked someone where to hustle?"

"How else was I going to find out?"

In *A Consumer's Guide to Male Hustlers* (pp. 92-96), I have written at length about the dynamics of agreeing on specific sex acts with an escort. It is based on what he will perform (or allow to be performed), what the client wants, and how much money will be exchanged. But with someone as inexperienced in sex work as Beauregard, a different scenario developed.

We had just started when Beauregard asked me seductively, "Will you come inside me? I really, really, need to get fucked."[1]

"Didn't your first john fuck you?"

"No. He wanted me to fuck *him*."

"Did you do it?"

"I had to."

Pleasing the sex worker and enjoying oneself simultaneously is a devoutly wished-for consummation. I do not care much for being a top, but I wanted to make Beauregard happy. As I screwed him, I had the feeling that what Beauregard asks for, Beauregard gets— maybe not from the Navy, but certainly from his sex partners.

Beauregard turned out to be a skillful sex worker in spite of his inexperience. His enjoyment of being penetrated was genuine. Both of us had a good time and we liked each other. When we were done, we lay in bed talking. He told me about his life before San Diego. "In North Carolina, I went to a Fundamentalist college. I was thinking of becoming a preacher. As you know, they aren't crazy about gays. They didn't like me much after they found out. That's when I joined the Navy."

"And they also aren't happy with homosexuals."

"I never told the Navy I was gay. I said they played too rough."

I changed the subject. "What is your ethnic background, Beauregard?"

"On my father's side I am Cajun. On my mother's, I am half Mexican and half American Indian."

I could see traces of all these ethnic groups in Beauregard. His facial features were broad, his lively eyes brown. His somewhat curly hair was dark brown and his complexion was fair. "I don't like my nose," he said.

"Why?"

"It's strange-looking."

I looked at his nose critically. Beauregard's observation was accurate. Somehow, his nose was out of proportion with the rest of his face—slightly too wide or too thick. But I didn't think it was a big deal. "One day soon, I'll have plastic surgery to fix it," he assured me.

It was close to ten p.m. when we started dressing. "Where am I taking you?"

"I'm tired. I need to crash."

"Where are you staying?"

"The first night I walked the streets. Next morning, I found john number one. With the money he gave me I paid a fleabag for one day. My stuff is still in a locker at the Greyhound. With your money I can pay the hotel tonight. But it won't leave me much money for eating."

I forgot to ask Beauregard where he was staying when I picked him up. Experience had taught me that it was not wise to spend the night with a newly found street hustler. By morning he, as well as sundry valuable household items, might disappear. But I liked Beauregard and wanted to help him. By allowing him to spend the night with me, he would save money for the next day. Against my better judgment, I invited him to stay the night. I didn't have to worry that Beauregard would want to crash at my place for more than one night. My ex would be back the next day.

Earlier, when we arrived at my place, I asked Beauregard whether he wanted a bite to eat. He said that he wasn't hungry. After extending my invitation for the night, Beauregard confessed that he had not eaten since breakfast. I fed him and we hit the sack. We slept in separate beds. I considered him my houseguest; I had not engaged his services for the night.

In the morning, after breakfast, I told Beauregard, "My ex and I will continue living together for the next three months. I can meet you here only on Fridays, early in the afternoon. I'm free at that time and my ex is still at work. I don't want to lose touch with you. Will you phone me Thursday evening? I'll be waiting for your call."

"Your ex won't mind?"

"No, he knows all about me and hustlers. We're parting on good terms. I just don't want to do it in his face."

When Beauregard called me Thursday evening, I invited him for lunch on Friday. Taking sex workers out for lunch or dinner is not unusual. It makes the planned sex session more "genteel"—the beginning or culmination of a successful date rather than a "crass commercial transaction." I had done this many times before meeting Beauregard and am still doing it nowadays. As I have written in Chapter 4, sometimes sex workers manage to talk clients into paying them for the time they spend at the meal. I am happy to invite a sex worker for a meal but will never compensate him for out-of-bed time.

Having lunch together on Fridays, before our sex session, became a tradition. By the fourth week, Beauregard had been successful enough in his new career to save money for a residential hotel right on Polk Street. Street sex workers with their own pads have a great advantage over their competitors. Less time is wasted traveling to and from clients' homes.

I became one of Beauregard's regulars, as well as a friend. I was attracted to his quirky personality and intelligence even more than his sexual performance. (In this respect, I preferred Lloyd and Alfonso.) It didn't take me long to realize that Beauregard was a charming, sexy, intelligent young guy who periodically screwed up big time.

Beauregard believed in miracles, as well he should have. When he needed money most, a check would arrive in the mail. In the beginning, I cashed his checks for him. I knew he was not making up stories. The first check was easy to understand. Beauregard liquidated his life-insurance policy. But other checks kept arriving, forwarded by his family in South Carolina: from the U.S. Navy, an inexplicable postdischarge benefit; from a court in North Carolina, a settlement he couldn't fully explain; and even from the Treasury Department for, as Beauregard put it, "believing in miracles."

In the fall of 1976, I moved into my own home and invited Beauregard to visit me. "You need somebody to clean for you," he told me, after surveying my fixer upper.

"I have been thinking about this lately."

"How about me doing it?"

"I don't know, Beauregard. Cleaning pays a lot less than hustling and is harder work. At least I think so."

"This is true. But I'm trying to find legitimate work. House cleaning may be fun for a while."

We agreed on his pay—a fraction of his hustling fee—and made a biweekly arrangement. Usually, I would not have allowed a hustler to clean my house, especially since I left the house as soon as Beauregard started working. But my relationship with him was not only that of client/sex worker. We were friends first; *and* he was also my sex worker *and* my housekeeper. I trusted him fully from our first meeting. Like everything else in his life, the housekeeper phase lasted only some six months.

Pretty soon Beauregard had his own apartment. He had an artistic touch and decorated it tastefully, if whimsically. A while later a cat appeared on the scene. He called her Jerusha, a good Old Testament name befitting a former preacher's pet. Like her owner, Jerusha also experienced miracles. In her kittenhood, her tail had been bitten off by a raccoon. Within a week of joining Beauregard's household, Jerusha tried to catch a bird and fell out of a third-floor window. She limped for the rest of her life but was otherwise healthy.

As Beauregard settled down domestically, he grew wilder sexually. When I visited him one day, he was wearing a pair of skimpy black leather shorts and a T-shirt with huge rips in it. On his feet he had shiny black boots. "Is the hustling business so bad that you can't afford a decent T-shirt?" I asked.

"This is my slave outfit."

"Are you playing S-and-M games these days?"

"Yes, it's the most exciting thing I've ever done. You know, a few nights ago I was having sex in the back of a truck. The dude blindfolded me and tied me to a post or something. Then I heard him rummaging in a drawer. It sounded like he was searching for a knife. Joseph, I was *so* scared! You know what happened?"

"Tell me."

"I came. Just by listening to the sound of the knives."

"And?"

"Oh, he whipped my ass some and then fucked me. The fun was really when I was blindfolded and scared shitless."

After playing "slave" for a few months, Beauregard tired of it. He enrolled in modeling school. While in training, he gave up his good-natured ways and became haughty. "Giving attitude is what modeling is all about," he informed me, pretending to take a turn on an imaginary stage. For a few weeks, he played the role of an imperious queen, treating everyone with grand hauteur. It didn't quite suit him. He was a lovable guy who always got his way. People accommodated him because they wanted to please him.

In the spring of 1977, I invited Beauregard to accompany me to a resort near Santa Cruz. "That's super," Beauregard said. "When do you want go?"

"How about Friday of next week?"

"You know that I'm having my plastic surgery on Monday next week? By Friday I'll be OK. It's going to be fun."

While still a modeling student, Beauregard had managed to talk San Francisco General into performing plastic surgery on his nose for free. He told them that he was depressed and only a nose job would make him mentally whole again.

"Are you sure that your face will have healed by then?" I asked.

"The doctor said it would take only a few days."

When I arrived at his apartment on Friday, a wide bandage covered his nose. It was secured behind his head. The rest of his face was puffy and bruised. "Are you sure you want to go like this?"

"I'm OK. Don't worry. We'll have sex one way or another."

"How will I do that without bending your new nose out of shape?"

"We don't need to be face to face."

I had not screwed Beauregard for quite a while. Now there wouldn't be any other choice.

I don't recall why I had picked this particular resort. The surroundings were pretty, but it catered mostly to aged yentas. In this straight environment we made an odd couple. I was a man in his late forties, accompanied by a twenty-one-year-old youth who looked as if he belonged in a hospital. Naturally, many ladies asked Beauregard solicitously why his face was bandaged. He gave the same answer: "Oh, I had a nose job a few days ago."

"Why, young man?" some of them asked.

"Because I want to look pretty."

I was embarrassed by Beauregard's answer to their questions. In my book, men were supposed to be ruggedly handsome, not *pretty*. (Paradoxically, I myself prefer to sleep with pretty guys, not rugged men.) But Beauregard was completely without guile. He blurted out whatever came to his head. In no time, he became the darling of the resort. The women happily swapped nose-job stories with him. Nobody paid attention to me.

How did his nose come out? After the swelling was gone, it looked the same to me.

As Beauregard grew older, his acne disappeared, leaving only slight scars. He also had his teeth straightened. In his middle twenties, he was almost handsome. I liked and enjoyed Beauregard, but I was never smitten with him. Those who had the misfortune of falling in love with him suffered a lot because he changed boyfriends every other year. (Once he took a break from lovers and went back to sex work for a few months.)

If I remember correctly, all his boyfriends, except the last one, were called "Jerry." Beauregard presented me to each new lover with the same introductory phrase: "Jerry, I want you to meet Joseph. I used to be his little prostitute." Without fail, as a new lover was phased in, the incumbent continued serving for a few months. Then Beauregard would arrange a ceremonial meeting between the incoming and the outgoing paramour. All previous lovers remained Beauregard's friends. His newest mate would be stuck with all the former consorts and even a john from the old times.

From my experience, whether escorts remain friends with former clients after they cease being sex workers depends entirely on how they felt about the job during the time they provided their services. They may have liked a particular client and enjoyed his company, but if being around him evokes memories of an unpleasant interval in their past, they will shun his company. If, on the other hand, they think that their sex-working days were a hoot, they will sometimes stay friends with their favorite clients.

When Beauregard told his lovers that he had been my "little prostitute," neither he nor they considered him a "hustling survivor." If Beauregard could tell the U.S. Navy to fuck off, he would have been able to handle any and all sex clients.

I stayed friends with only a few former sex workers. I often wonder whether Michael and I will still remain friends after we stop being sex worker and client. We have been seeing each other for over three years, sometimes twice a week. We genuinely like each other as people; neither one of us could have faked it over such a long stretch of time. However, my gut feeling is that without the sex component our friendship is likely to fall apart. It has worked quite well in the context of sex work. But Michael really does not like "escorting," even though it affords him a lifestyle he would never have been able to attain solely from his other jobs. As escorting goes, he doesn't mind doing it with me. I know that he much prefers me over better-paying gentlemen. But to him, I will always represent a john whom he "escorted," reminding him of his sex-working days. Among Michael's better qualities is his loyalty to his friends. Breaking our friendship will, no doubt, pose a dilemma for him.

Beauregard was a different case. From our first meeting in front of the St. Francis Hotel, I was just a person he happened to like. True, he sex-worked for me and cleaned my house for a while. As I have written in Chapter 3, it is all about attitude—how the sex worker views himself as a service provider.

Modern sex workers, with their fancy ads, are an unheroic lot as compared to their progenitors, the street hustlers. Among the latter, one found gold nuggets scattered in the sand. Earlier I wrote about one such hustler, Terry, the powerful witch, who eventually became a computer pro. He did so without any formal schooling. Beauregard was a similar success story. For a few months he attended classes at a skills center and learned word processing. A year later, he became a legal assistant and swiftly advanced to office supervisor.

He also joined various groups of the human growth potential movement. From simply believing in miracles, he became "empowered" to "manifest," to "create," and sometimes even to "source." He felt invincible, and for a few years he was.

In the middle 1990s, I was involved for a while with an HIV-*negative* support group. The younger members were jealous of the older generation. Naively they believed that before the advent of AIDS, San Francisco was a gay-sex paradise where men screwed around merrily and where sexually transmitted diseases were unknown. In reality, a multitude of health scares existed then, although they were not as catastrophic.

When Beauregard was still my housekeeper, he arrived one day dragging his left leg. "My knee hurts so much," he said. "This has been going on for over a week."

"You should see a doctor," I told him.

"I'm going to my shaman tomorrow. He does moxibustion on my knee."

"What does that mean?"

"He burns moxa on my skin."

"And what is 'moxa'?"

"The shaman puts stuff on your skin and burns it. He calls it an antiagent. He'll do it on my bad knee."

"Doesn't it hurt?"

"A little bit. But later you feel so much better."

When Beauregard arrived two weeks later, he could barely negotiate the stairs. "Beauregard, you must see a doctor. Forget about cleaning house. I'll drive you to San Francisco General."

"But my shaman said his moxibustion treatments take a while to kick in." He winced in pain as he spoke.

"Have it your own way, or your shaman's way. I still believe I should drive you to the hospital."

I went shopping for groceries. When I came back, Beauregard was sitting on the floor crying. "The pain is killing me, Joseph."

"I am taking you to the hospital right now, and that's it."

We waited in line at triage in the hospital's emergency room. When Beauregard's turn came, the RN asked a few routine questions, and then, "Have you had a venereal disease lately?"

"Yes. Gonorrhea."

"When?"

"Six . . . no, eight weeks ago.

"Where?"

"In my rectum. I was treated at the VD clinic."

Why, I thought to myself, does everything in San Francisco revolve around sex? Beauregard wasn't even complaining about his rectum.

I left him in the hospital because it was going to take at least four hours before Beauregard would be examined by a doctor. I was not the least bit surprised about his gonorrhea. It happened regularly to many people I knew. It was regarded much less seriously than the flu. Treatment was just two shots of penicillin—one of which was fairly painful. Syphilis was taken more seriously, which was probably due to the violent reaction after the initial syphilis penicillin treatment.

It turned out that Beauregard's gonorrhea had not been treated adequately and had developed into arthritis. The hospital took care of it, though Beauregard's knee hurt for a long while. A year later, Beauregard came down with hepatitis A. Then he had to be treated for anal warts, and again later for gonorrhea. And so it went. Long before AIDS, many diseases existed in the gay community. However, they were regarded as a nuisance rather than as a real threat to one's physical well-being.[2]

Beauregard's sexually transmitted diseases were not a result of his sex work. As far as I remember, he caught most of them after giving up escorting. Following the usual pattern, he had much more time and sexual energy once he had stopped escorting and was free of clients.

In the late 1980s I lost touch with Beauregard. From a mutual acquaintance I learned that Beauregard had bought a house in El Cerrito, a forty-five-minute car ride from San Francisco. "Where did he get the money to buy a house?" I asked.

"He tripped over some wire or something at another law firm. He was represented by the lawyers of his own office. The settlement was good enough to buy a house."

"How badly was he hurt?"

"Not much, as far as I know. But he has AIDS."

I felt numb. So many of my friends and acquaintances in those days had the disease. It would have been a miracle if Beauregard had somehow been spared.

I phoned him at the number his friend had given me. The message on the answering machine said that he was out of town. A month later, Beauregard called me from San Francisco. "I'm spending the day in the city with all my doctors before flying to Yugoslavia. If you're free, let's do lunch."

"I'll make time, Beauregard. Why are you going to Yugoslavia?"

"Remember, Joseph, that I used to tell you that I believe in miracles?

"Yes."

"Well, I need to create one big miracle. I'll tell you about it at lunch."

Beauregard had lost a lot of weight but otherwise looked well. "I now live with Glenn. We're nonsexual lovers. You know that I have AIDS?"

"Yes."

"Well, maybe Our Lady of Medjogurje—I mean Medjugorje— will heal me. I am having problems with the pronunciation of her name."

"Who's she?"

"It's like Lourdes and St. Bernadette. I found out about it only last month. In Medjugorje, the Virgin appears to some pilgrims; others just feel her presence. But even that is enough to be cured. You can't imagine what a hassle it is to travel in my condition. And if the Yugoslavs discover that I have AIDS, they won't let me in."

"But you're not even Catholic."

"Our Lady of Medjugorje is an equal-opportunity healer!"

"Well, I wish you a bon voyage and I will pray that Our Lady of Medjugorje heals you." I almost started crying. I had been losing so many friends to AIDS. I knew in my heart that Beauregard would be the next to go.

He called me when he returned. He sounded only mildly upbeat. "The Virgin didn't appear to me, but I did feel her presence. I'm a bit better, though I'm still tired from the trip."

Two months went by. One morning the phone rang. Glenn, Beauregard's "nonsexual" lover, was on the line. "Beauregard wants to say good-bye to his friends. He's in the hospital."

"How's he doing?"

"Very poorly. He'll leave us in a few days. Will you visit him?"

"Of course."

Beauregard had lost even more weight. Though his face was gaunt, it had not changed much. "Hi, Joseph. Meet Glenn, my lover, and my friend Timothy. Guys, this is Joseph. I used to be his little prostitute."

It struck me as a pretty irreverent remark to make on one's own deathbed. But at least Beauregard remained true to form. Glenn probably knew all about his past because he had no reaction to Beauregard's comment. Timothy looked somewhat shaken.

"See, Joseph," Beauregard said, and showed me a tube embedded in his chest, "this is what keeps me alive. The doctors gave up on me long ago. Every day of my life is a miracle."

A week later, Beauregard passed away in the arms of Glenn, his "nonsexual" lover.

Chapter 9

Defaulting to Sex Work

In Chapter 5, I told of my search for a masseur (eventually to become a permanent sex worker) as a replacement for Winston. To date, my search has been unsuccessful. The guys I have tried out were unschooled massage practitioners, often with a clumsy touch. The masseurs who took me up on my suggestion to substitute sexual enhancements for the labor-intensive massage didn't turn me on much. The ones who excited me physically were willing to offer only token enhancements—for instance, a peck on the cheek instead of French kissing.

For practical reasons, I try to set up my appointments with new masseurs or escorts by contacting them the day before I want to see them. They answer their pager or voice mail when they get around to it: immediately, within an hour, half a day later, or never. Sometimes by the end of an afternoon of unanswered calls, all I have to show for my efforts is a list of ten masseurs I *tried* contacting. This is tedious and frustrating work. By giving myself twenty-four hours lead time, I am not forced to make an appointment with the one masseur who answers his phone in person.

One afternoon I started my search with an advertiser who described himself as a "Dreamy Erotic Creole." I believed he was a good candidate with whom to inaugurate my search. Surprisingly, he answered in person. He sounded disinterested and somewhat gruff. I am extremely sensitive to voices and was immediately turned off. I terminated the conversation under some pretext. Even though the masseur called me back, using his dial-back feature, I honored my intuition. To be fair, I may have awakened him from a siesta, or he may have been annoyed by a previous jerk-off nut. But from long experience I have learned never to use logic to overrule my intuition.

The next ad I answered read:

> Vietnamese pleasure boy 28 for playful and relaxing nude massage. Call Van, $50, out only [followed by a phone number].

It was an expensive ad, set in large print with a border. To me, it indicated that Van was doing well in his massage business. The style of the ad also suggested that Van was an imaginative person. As requested by his pager's voice mail, I punched in my own number.

Before I had a chance to make another call, my phone rang. "Hello," the caller said, "my name is V-A-N." He spelled out the letters of his name.

"Hi, Van," I answered, "my name is Joseph. Please tell me a bit about yourself."

Van spoke laboriously and deliberately with a heavy Vietnamese accent. Every fifth word or so he spelled out to make certain that I understood it. I was on the verge of disqualifying Van because I was not in the market for just a single massage session. In the long run, I did not see how Van and I could hold meaningful conversations before or after our sex sessions. But in spite of Van's cumbersome speech, I got good vibes from his voice. Just to make certain, I asked him whether he would give me a "release massage." He understood my question perfectly, didn't spell out any words, and assured me that he would, indeed, give me a "full-body, release massage."

If sex workers do not have their own transportation, I prefer picking them up in the Castro District. It makes it easier for them, and it allows me to "preview" them before they are on the threshold of my home. Explaining to Van where he should wait for me was a painfully slow process. He seemed to be taking notes on my instructions and repeated them carefully, often spelling out this or that word. I'll say this for him: he was a good speller. The next day he called me at the appointed time. He was not where we had agreed upon but, rather, at "N-O-E Street and Market."

"Why are you at N-O-E and Market and not at Castro and Nineteenth?" By now *I* was spelling out words.

"I'm very hungry. My first food today. I'm in restaurant on N-O-E and Market eating food. Can you come to N-O-E Street at seven-thirty?"

I was miffed. Van should have eaten on his own time. Also, it had taken me a good ten minutes to explain to Van where to meet me in the Castro. Now we had to do it all over again. "Do you know where the L-I-B-R-A-R-Y on N-O-E and Market is? You can see a flagpole there."

"Flagpole" was not a good word to use. Even spelling it out did not help. But Van was calling from a public phone and by looking around he spotted the library. "OK," he said, "I see the L-I-B-R-A-R-Y. You come seven-thirty?"

"OK, Van. I'll see you there."

As I pulled into the library's parking lot, I saw Van. He was dressed neatly and professionally. His shirt, sweater, and pants were white. He was much older than his advertised age, but I had expected this. Van was thin, bordering on gaunt, and of medium height. To my eye he looked rather sexy. As he got into the car I was almost overwhelmed by the tobacco smell emanating from him. It hadn't bothered me in the past, but I was no longer accustomed to it. His first words were, "I'm sorry about change. I eat S-T-E-A-K in restaurant. I'm very hungry. My first food today."

"Why didn't you eat earlier?"

"Because I have no money. After number one customer, B-R-U-C-E, only I have money to eat food."

"So, Joseph," I mused to myself, "With all your experience, you have managed to come up with a starving masseur." Still, I felt comfortable with Van.

As massages by untrained "releasers" go, I gave Van a passing grade. He had a good touch and did not skip this or that limb. While he worked, he told me about himself. He not only spelled out names; he had a thing about addresses. J-A-M-E-S, for instance, lived at 5-7-6 L-A-R-K-I-N Street. He was also meticulous about degrees of kinship. He came from a family with *many* siblings and made sure that I knew that some were only his *step*brothers and *step*sisters. I tuned out most of what he had to say but, subconsciously, caught the spelled-out names and precise addresses of various charities offering shelter to the homeless. By the time Van was working on my feet, I understood that he was homeless.

The miracle of pagers! As long as Van was willing to spend thirty-five cents to call back the phone number displayed on the screen of his beeper, his clients would never know that he was homeless. Fifteen years after giving up Polk Street, I was back to vagrant hustlers, albeit with impressive ads.

At the end of the massage, Van snuggled next to me and hugged me tenderly. Then, very quickly and expertly, he "released" me. It was obvious that he had a lot of experience performing this maneuver. When we were done, he asked permission to use the shower. This explained how he was so clean. He had already massaged B-R-U-C-E today and must have taken a shower there.

When he was dressed, he asked me shyly whether he could make a phone call to A-L-E-X. He had called him a number of times earlier and wasted money listening to his voice mail message. If A-L-E-X answered in person, he would go there and, in return for helping him paint, stay the night at his place.

"You do painting jobs?" I asked Van.

"Yes, also many small jobs. I can also do G-A-R-D-E-N-I-N-G. Also, I can stay your home and watch when you go away. I'm very honest."

"How much do you charge per hour for small jobs?"

"What you will give me."

"No, Van. I need to know how much you charge per hour."

"A donation. What you give me is OK." He didn't spell out "donation."

I have written extensively about Van because he is a good illustration of male escorts and masseurs who do sex work by default. They are not professional sex workers providing their clients an awesome sensual experience. They do their sex thing for a number of reasons only vaguely related to their clients' needs. They prostitute themselves, first, because they are able to do it, and are roughly within an acceptable age bracket; second, because it will make more money for them than a low-paying job; and third, because it may lead to good future prospects.

Van has been in this country for fourteen years, working at this or that job, from New York City to Anchorage. The few times he had a real home was when he was a live-in sex partner. Unlike all other jobs, massage work literally opened doors for Van. In my particular case, I would have hired him to do odd jobs around the house. (Two months later his pager number had been disconnected. Van had probably moved to another city.)

Paradoxically, relationships with the Vans of this world can develop into friendships much more easily than with professional sex workers. Workers such as Van do not follow a sex workers' manual. They have no preconceived notions of how they *should* interact with their clients. Consequently, they are open to innovative arrangements that will benefit both them and their clients—all of which brings me to the story of Billy Fu, the hero of this chapter.

* * *

I met Billy in the early 1980s on Polk Street while cruising for a hustler. He was a short, thin, and plain-looking guy. He appeared to be of Asian extraction, though I could not precisely place his ethnic background. He would not have been my first or even second choice, had these been available. On that particular evening, he was the only hustler on the street who matched my minimum physical requirements. It was him or nobody. So I spoke to him. I found out that his name was Billy and that he was twenty-two years old. "Are you working tonight?" I asked.

"Do you mean, 'Am I hustling?'"

"Yes."

"I'm hustling, but I'm not a hustler."

"This is deep, Billy. Please explain."

"Let's talk about it later."

Judging by the way he spoke English, he was born in the United States or came here as a young child. I was not terribly attracted to him, but the more we talked the better I liked his personality. It did not take us long to strike a deal.

"Let's go to my place," Billy suggested.

It is always less trouble to go to the sex worker's place because one does not have to drive him back home after the session is over. As I have already noted, it is also much safer. But some workers live in pretty shabby hotel rooms. Billy seemed to read my mind. "Don't worry—I live in a nice apartment."

"Where?"

"On Bush and Octavia."

"OK, Billy. You know what? Let's walk to your place. It's not too far. I don't want to look for another parking space again this evening."

"We can go in my car. *I* never have parking problems. I'll drive you back to your car when we finish."

I was impressed. It is extremely rare for street hustlers to have their own transportation. Billy's car was parked down the block. In my opinion, he had parked too close to a fire hydrant but there was no ticket on the windshield. I can't recall the make of his car, but I remember that it was white, sporty, and recent.

"What is your ethnic background, Billy?" I asked once he started driving.

"I am an adopted child. I know that I have Chinese and Hawaiian blood."

"Where were you raised?"

"In San Francisco. My parents live here."

It was a short drive. Billy parked his car. "See, my apartment is across the street," he said, pointing to a large building.

This time he parked right in front of a hydrant. "Billy, you can't park here legally."

"I never worry about things like that," he answered.

Billy lived in a split-level, one-bedroom apartment. The downstairs living room was sparsely furnished. In one corner, right on the floor, stood a terrarium. Coiled on the bottom was a thick snake with brownish skin. "Meet Kamehameha, my pet rubber boa."

"Not a boa constrictor?"

"Kamehameha here is a *rubber* boa. This is the correct name for my snake."

I went over to say hello to the rubber boa, hoping that I would not be asked to pet it. Fortunately, Billy motioned me to sit on the couch. The rent for Billy's apartment must have been high. It bespoke of financial stability, not street prostitution. "You told me that you hustle but are not a hustler. What did you mean by this?"

"I only hustle when I need the money. This is not what I do for a living."

"What sort of work do you do?"

"I can do anything I put my mind to. My last job was selling computers."

"What happened?"

"The boss hated me because I knew more about computers than him. He fired me."

"What other work have you done?"

"I'm a handyman, a painter. I do gardening, and I can fix appliances."

"I need handymen in my life even more than hustlers. I may have some work for you. Where did you learn all of these skills? Did you go to a vocational school?

"No, all I got is a GED. I spent a lot of time in juvy."

I knew that juvy was an abbreviation for juvenile hall, where delinquent children are tried and sometimes incarcerated for brief periods. Many street hustlers are juvy graduates.

Billy took me to his small upstairs bedroom. As I recall, the only pieces of furniture were a bed and a chair. When Billy removed his clothes, I saw a large scar on the back of his thigh. It looked like a burn.

"When did that happen?" I asked Billy, pointing to his right thigh.

"When I was a little boy. My father burned me with an iron skillet."

My facial expression must have given away my feelings. "It wasn't a big deal. My father sometimes has a bad temper. I spent a year in a foster home after he burned me."

"How do you get along with your parents these days?"

"More or less OK. My father pays my rent here. You know that I live with a lover?"

"No. Who's he?"

"Ralph, a blond boy. He's a year younger than me, and he's a bit messed up." With his left index finger Billy pointed to his forehead to indicate that Ralph had mental problems. "He does drugs all the time. But we've been together now for one year."

"Does he know that you hustle?"

"He hustles, too. But usually he is too spaced out to make money."

"Where's he tonight?"

"I sent him out to a bar."

"Do you also do drugs?"

"Never! I hate the stuff."

Billy was not the greatest sex worker, though he performed what had been promised. This included everything but penetration either way, which he had told me he wouldn't do. He endeared himself to me because, like me, he enjoyed long conversations in bed. Billy and I clicked instantly as companions. The sex was thrown in as a bonus.

I had an incredible experience in Billy's bedroom that night. As he was talking about his childhood, an unrelated image suddenly popped into my head. "I bet you have a knife under your mattress," I interrupted him.

"Get off the bed for a moment," Billy said. He lifted the mattress. Sure enough, under it was a knife, with a blade some eight inches long. "In this business you can't be too careful," Billy said, as he readjusted the mattress. He didn't ask me how I knew about the knife. Had he asked, I would not have been able to answer.

After sex, still lying in bed, I asked Billy, "Would you like to come to my house next week? I want to ask you a few questions about the garden and my appliances. Then we can turn a trick."

"Sure. How about a week from today?"

"OK. Come before sunset to look at my garden. I'll order a pizza for supper and then we'll have sex."

It was winter so we agreed on 4:00 p.m. the following Tuesday.

It had taken close to three hours before we were back on the street. Naturally, there was a ticket on Billy's windshield. Briefly, he studied it. Then he tore it into little pieces in front of me, scattering them on the sidewalk. "This is what I do with this garbage."

Billy is a wonderful guy, but there is a screw lose in his head, I mused to myself. My instant diagnosis of Billy's condition still holds true today and has been corroborated by medical authorities. He and his off-and-on boyfriend, Ralph, are alive and well, both diligently collecting SSI due to their mental states.

The following Tuesday, I waited for Billy from four to seven at night. Then I gave up on him and went out to do some shopping. When I returned, half an hour later, a car was parked in my driveway. The driver saw me and stepped out. It was dark, but I recognized Billy. He was holding a heavy-duty flashlight. "What took you so long?" he asked.

I was furious. "What took *you* so long? You were supposed to be here at four."

"Ralph let Kamehameha escape from his cage. We had to search for him through the building."

"Why didn't you call me?"

"Have you ever had to search for an escaped rubber boa snake?"

"No. Where did you find him?"

"In his cage. Ralph was tweaking and didn't see the snake under the newspaper."

"Come into the house," I told Billy.

Once we were inside, I asked him, "What is the flashlight for?"

"Didn't you want me to look at your garden?"

"During daylight. Not in the dark, Billy."

"With the flashlight it won't be dark."

Feeling like a complete fool, I led Billy into the garden. Shining his flashlight while inspecting the garden thoroughly, Billy proclaimed, "I need to come back and do some pruning for you. I also think some of your shrubs should be transplanted."

"Do you think you would be able do this work during *daylight* hours?"

Billy was impervious to my sarcasm, because he replied, "It's better to do gardening in daylight. I'll come another day and will take care of it."

"How much will you charge me?"

"It's not a big deal. I'll do it as a favor."

We went back into the house. "Didn't you want me to look at some of your appliances?"

I had forgotten about this part. Billy went to his car and brought back a large toolbox. With great dexterity he performed minor repairs. He promised to fix a wiring problem when he did the garden.

We had a leisurely sex session, talking about this and that. I enjoyed my conversation with Billy. He was a street philosopher of sorts. Before he left, Billy made an appointment with me for the gardening. It took three failed attempts before it was done.

Van had the potential of becoming another Billy in my life. Probably a much more reliable version. But with Van I would not have been able to hold long conversations nor enjoy the companionship I had with Billy. What these two had in common was that they defaulted to prostitution when they needed cash in a hurry.

Separate from our sex sessions, Billy and I exchanged favors. He parked his car in my garage for extended periods when it faced being towed away for the unpaid tickets it had amassed. He, in turn, was my handyman on call. Let me rephrase this: He was a free handyman I *could* call. Half the time my calls went unanswered. But when he fixed something, it was always well done.

Billy hated hustling on Polk Street. However, he had great difficulties cultivating regulars because he failed to keep his appointments.

Often, when a regular did try to reach him by phone to make an appointment, the line would be disconnected for nonpayment. As a result, when Billy was short of money, he would take initiative and call former clients. Without polite exchanges, he would come right to the point: "I need some money real bad. Let's turn a trick today, OK?" If the answer was no, Billy would add, "But I haven't eaten for a whole day. I *need* the money."

I had introduced Billy to a friend of mine, and he used Billy's services a few times. Then my friend tired of being stood up by Billy and dropped him. When Billy called him out of the blue because he was hungry, my friend said to him, "If you own a grocery store you don't open it just when you happen to need money. You have to be there all the time to take care of your customers. If you hustle, you also have to be there for your johns when they want to see you, not just when you need their money."

"Your friend is real weird," Billy told me when he saw me a few weeks later. "He thinks I hustle because I enjoy doing it."

Patiently, I tried to explain to Billy the parable of the grocery store, but he never got it. Why would he hustle when he didn't need to? Why would a customer refuse to turn a trick with Billy when he was hungry?

For a few years, Billy and I went out socially as friends. I was aware that he sometimes made cameo appearances on Polk Street when he was hard up for cash. I didn't give any thought to what would happen if Billy ran into a client while in my company. One day, I took him to a potluck picnic sponsored by an Asian-Caucasian social organization.

Once we joined the picnic, Billy and I separated on purpose. He wanted to meet a "blond boy," and I was focused on cruising a young, cute Asian man. My prospects were much brighter than Billy's. For mysterious reasons, such organizations invariably attract older Caucasians and younger "ethnics."

I was standing in the buffet line when Wolfgang slithered up to me. A moment earlier he wasn't anywhere near me. Wolfgang was known by one and all as the biggest gossip in the organization. "Who's the Asian you brought with you?"

"His name is Billy. Billy Fu."

"Do you know what sort of work he does?"

"He's into computers, but he was laid off. Now he finds jobs here and there. Last month he painted the outside of my house." This much was true. I didn't mention that Billy arrived so late in the day that he had to finish the job at night, rigging up floodlights.

"That's all you know about what Billy does for a living?"

"If you need a good painter, hire Billy. He'll do a good job for you."

"He's a *street* hustler. Hangs out on Polk Street. I wouldn't be seen *dead* with him." Just as Wolfgang had materialized out of nowhere, he dematerialized into the ether.

I didn't say anything to Billy until the end of the picnic. We had driven in his car. Once he pulled out of the parking lot, I asked him, "Do you know that some people in the organization don't like you?"

"Yes. Probably Wolfgang. What did he tell you?"

"He said that you hustled on Polk Street."

"Did he also tell you that I turned him down?"

"No. Why did you turn him down?"

"Because he's a jerk."

"Meaning?"

"He's such an asshole. We'd met at The Giraffe a month earlier and he tried to pick me up. I turned him down then. When I was prostituting on Polk, he wanted me to come home with him and I told him to get lost."

Naturally, Wolfgang spread the word that I had brought a hustler to the picnic. Members had seen me before with cute partners. Now they understood the secret of my "success." As a result, I became more popular with some and lost face with many others.

Neither Billy nor I gave much thought to the complexity of our relationship. It did not faze me that one day Billy would paint my house; the next day, we would go out for lunch; and a week later, he would call and ask me if he "could hustle for me." By gay society standards, he was primarily a *hustler.* In the process, it overshadowed all of his other attributes. One did not bring the likes of him to potlucks. Ironically, postmodern sex workers would also consider my social activities with Billy inappropriate, *unless* he was paid for every minute of his time.

Chapter 10

Sugar Daddies
and Their Ungrateful Sons

Omar came into my life four years ago through a personal ad I had placed in a freebie San Francisco publication. My headline read: "Generous Sr. ISO Jr. MOC." The ISO stands for "in search of," and the MOC for "man of color." "Generous" is the code word for "willing to pay." In the text of the ad, I stated that I was a "mentor type."

On the phone, Omar told me that he needed a mentor. I have mentored him well—maybe even too well. Following is Omar's saga.

When I opened the door to admit Omar on his first visit, I saw before me a well-proportioned short guy, five-feet, five-inches at most, with light brown skin and, judging from his open shirt, little or no body hair. The color of his eyes was very dark, almost black, contrasting with the much lighter brown shade of his soft, long, curly hair. In the lobe of his left ear he wore a gold earring the size of a dime. He had an intense look about him, mitigated somewhat by his friendly smile. The nails on his left hand were painted dark green. I am a much more conventional person than I would prefer to be. Omar's nail polish unsettled me. The first words I blurted out were, "Why are your nails painted green?"

"This is in fashion nowadays. They used to be navy blue."

Omar was not one for small talk. Five minutes into the visit he told me the bizarre story of his emigration from North Africa to San Francisco. He was born in 1975 in Tangier, Morocco, on the African side of the Strait of Gibraltar. He is the illegitimate son of a Moroccan father, whose name he does not know, and Dolores Leticia Nuñez, his Spanish mother. His parents named him Omar, which is commonplace both in Arabic and Spanish. A year after Omar's birth, Dolores left his father and moved to Algeciras, Spain, on the European side of the Strait. There she met an American tourist, Charles Goodwin. She married him in Algeciras and, after the she obtained her immigration papers, moved to Poughkeepsie, New York, with her new husband and her infant son. Omar remembers little of this. His first real boyhood memories are from the Mission District in San Francisco, living in a small, decrepit apartment with his newly divorced mother, now called Mrs. Dolores Goodwin.

Like many single mothers raising an only child, Dolores's relationship with Omar has been too intense. To this day, both mother and son fiercely love and resent each other. Keenly aware of the prejudices in Europe, and especially those in southern Spain against North Africans, Dolores fabricated a false identity for her son. Throughout his childhood, he believed himself to be of Basque origin, the son of an ETA (Basque terrorist) underground separatist killed by the Spanish police. His school documents list his birthplace as Bilbao, Spain, a major Basque city.

His mother chose an excellent cover for her son. In the predominantly Hispanic Mission District, little, if anything, was known about the Basques and their quarrel with the Spaniards. Dolores herself never bothered to learn much about the people of Omar's fictitious father. These lies were abruptly exposed when Omar, a ninth-grade student at the time, started working on a school assignment, "My Ethnic Roots." With a teenager's passion for the truth, he ferreted out his real roots. To the great dismay of his mother, he immediately declared himself an African from Morocco, discarding his Spanish heritage.

As soon as Omar unburdened himself of his false origins, he brought up a second issue to set the record straight about his sexuality. "When we spoke on the phone, I forgot to tell you that I'm bisexual and have a girlfriend. For relationships, I like women better—for sex I prefer men. Does this bother you?"

"Not at all. Tell me about your girlfriend."

"We aren't really dating all that seriously, though Annette believes I'm her boyfriend. I like hanging out with her and she's a good fuck. I'm too busy, too young, to make commitments."

"On the phone you told me that you were twenty-one and a student at SF State. Did I get this right?"

"Yes. I'm twenty-one. I'll turn twenty-two in three months."

"What are you taking up at college?"

"When I started, at nineteen, I wanted to become a high school teacher, maybe teach math and music. Things got all twisted around. Now my major is English. I don't know what I'll do with it once I graduate.

"And when will that be?"

"In two years. I suppose I can earn a modest living playing the guitar and singing folk songs in cafés. I have made some money doing gigs. I'm not a great artist, though. The trouble is, I don't really know what I want. . . . You know, politically, I'm to the far left. But I also want money, lots and lots of it."

"Did you answer my ad because of the 'generous' or the 'mentor'?"

"Both. I suppose I like the company of older men, not necessarily sexually, because I grew up without a father."

Omar had called me from his car's cellular phone to set up our meeting. Much of the time we could barely hear each other. We did establish that both of us were HIV negative, but we did not have a chance to discuss our sexual likes and dislikes. I had no idea what Omar liked to do in bed. Now that I saw him in person, I was quite attracted to him. His greatest asset was his tremendous sexual magnetism. It occurred to me that both men and women could easily fall under his spell. Inexplicably, I was afraid that we wouldn't be compatible sexually. It was just an intuitive hunch that things wouldn't work out. Usually, my intuition in these matters turns out to be correct. "Let me make a suggestion, Omar," I told him. "Why don't we try out having sex. Whatever happens, I'll pay you fifty dollars."

"OK. I've never been paid for sex before."

"Had you thought about doing it before you answered my ad?"

"Many, many times. It has been a constant fantasy of mine."

Omar had a firm little body. His circumcised cock, of medium size, was as solid as his body. As soon as we lay down, Omar had a full erection. I took him into my arms and tried kissing him. He averted his face. "I kiss only women," he said.

Since kissing is a very big deal for me, I felt deflated. "What do you like doing, Omar?" I asked.

"Fuck you. Safely, of course, with a condom."

"Omar, I don't get fucked. What else do you have in your repertoire?"

Omar appeared bewildered by my question. "I screw, Joseph. I screw men and women and transsexuals and gays, and I am really good at what I do."

"You're doing your countrymen proud."

"What do you mean?"

"From my reading, I'm sure that most Moroccan men feel exactly as you do—a man's mission in life is to screw women and, if need be, queers."

"Exactly," Omar said, without thinking. Then he caught himself. "But you've put it rather crudely."

We tried various other sexual maneuvers but they turned Omar off and didn't excite me. In the end, I barely managed to climax by dry humping him. Omar, though, by just using his hand, came quickly and abundantly right after me. I was disappointed that things didn't work out between us. I would have liked Omar to become one of my regular sex workers.

After we dressed, we went back to the living room and talked. Omar was intelligent, chatty, and amusing. We had many common interests. Although I didn't desire to have sex with him again, I wanted to remain friends. "Changing the subject completely, Omar," I said, "obviously, we're not compatible sexually. But I would like to keep you as a friend. How do you feel about it?"

"Why wouldn't we be friends?"

"Because, Omar, usually 'escorts' are not seeking unpaid friendships."

"I like you, too. I need a mentor. And you can also teach me how to become a successful hustler."

Omar's fascination with sex work went much deeper than just the money he could make from it. More than anything else, there was the thrill and adventure of screwing another man *and* getting paid for it. Against my advice, he went to a hustler bar on Polk Street the next day. There he was picked up by a middle-aged man whom he screwed in the back of the john's station wagon. Omar made a cool $100 in less than an hour. He was elated. He liked to penetrate, enjoyed the adulation of the "screwee," and was richer for the experience. Far from feeling sullied by prostituting himself, he sounded triumphant when he told me about his adventure.

I suggested that he run an escort ad in one of San Francisco's gay weeklies and also insert a free "seeking generous man" personal in one of the freebie general publications. When we started composing the first ad, the question of his ethnicity came up. In my opinion, writing "Moroccan/Spanish" in the ad would be puzzling to potential clients. Omar could not really describe himself as either Spanish or Moroccan. He is too dark to pass for a Spaniard and too European looking to be taken for a Moroccan. "When people ask you about your ethnic background, what do you say?"

"Ever since I've started telling people that I'm an African from Morocco, they think I'm bullshitting them."

"Did anybody ever question you when you told them that you were Basque?"

"Hell, no. Most people don't know anything about the Basques."

"Well, Omar?"

"What?"

"Maybe your mother was right—at least when it comes to escorting."

"Meaning?"

"You have to put a label on yourself in the ad. First and foremost, you can describe yourself as a 'young, handsome, total top.' But you should say something about your ethnicity."

"Why?"

"Because readers want to form a mental image of you before they answer your ad. The 'handsome total top' will attract a certain group of callers. If you don't mention a specific ethnic group, they'll assume that you're Caucasian. As a rule, advertisers who don't mention their ethnic group are considered to be white. When clients see you in person, they'll feel that you misled them. Since 'Basque' will mean little to most of them, it is your job to describe yourself accurately on the phone so they can visualize you in their mind's eye. If you happen to run into a client who has seen Basques before, you'll have to improvise."

Reluctantly, he agreed. "Now we have to find a working name for you," I said.

"What's wrong with Omar?"

"Nothing. It's a somewhat unusual name. With your stats in the ad as well as your real name, friends of yours might identify you. It's also more practical to have a working name. You know immediately what the call is about."

"If I have to lie about my ethnicity, then I don't want to add another falsehood with a fictitious name."

"You're breaking a sex workers' convention. But suit yourself."

The two-pronged advertising campaign I suggested to Omar produced quite different results. The paid ad was answered by clients who wanted to be topped by their escort. Some liked him well enough and engaged his services more than once. As soon as Omar got a handle on his new calling, he started raising his fee. Within three years, it went up from eighty dollars to one hundred and forty dollars, an increase well ahead of the Consumer Price Index.

The personal ad seeking a "generous mentor" brought in fewer but more interesting responses. A number of them came from men who didn't want to pay for sex in hard cash but were willing to take Omar on trips to faraway places or help him with his rent and tuition. I have to give Omar credit: Most sex workers wouldn't have bothered with such offers, especially from clients they didn't know well. Omar followed up on these contacts. Except for one case, nothing substantial came out of these meetings.

The one exception has been his affair with Marvin Katz, a psychiatrist. Marvin was smitten with Omar the moment he saw him. Even more so when he discovered that Omar was mildly turned on by his foot fetish. Many months later, he told Omar that other sex workers were bored or even turned off when he sucked on their toes and licked the soles of their feet. I suspect that Marvin's symbolic submissiveness appealed to the "top" aspect in Omar. "I screw Marvin every now and then," Omar said, "more to please myself than him. But even just pleasuring myself makes Marvin happy."

At their first meeting, Dr. Katz offered to become Omar's mentor and benefactor. Schooled by me, Omar believed that whatever else a client promised, he had to compensate an escort on a per-session basis. He took Marvin's offer under consideration, but made him pay the going rate like all other clients. Pretty soon, Marvin started using Omar's services twice weekly. After a few sessions, Marvin ordered in dinners from fancy restaurants for himself and his sex worker.

By then, Omar had befriended other sex workers. They told him that they charged by the hour, even if no sex was involved. Omar wanted to know my opinion on this point.

"Well, Omar," I asked, "do you like having dinner with Marvin?"

"Yeah. He's a nice man, likes music, and often has good ideas in his head. He isn't handsome but also not really ugly."

"Can you describe him?"

"He's fifty-two years old. Tall, thin, balding. He has pretty blue eyes, but his jaw is sort of pinched. And working out in a gym would be good for him."

"He's a psychiatrist. Does he have meaningful insights?"

"Certainly not into himself."

"Do you enjoy his company?"

"Yes, I do. Even if I didn't, I would put up with Marvin. He has the best marijuana in town."

Omar is a pothead. He has also done a lot of acid in his life. Because he is subject to extreme mood swings, I've suggested to him time and again to lay off drugs. He pooh-poohs my views on drugs, comparing me to Nancy Reagan, of all people.

"What you're telling me, Omar, is that you do enjoy being with Marvin out of bed. You're having a good time and all the pot you can smoke. He has become your 'regular.' Of course you shouldn't charge him by the hour."

After a few dinners at home, Marvin began taking Omar to elegant restaurants and, later in the evening, to a concert or the opera. At the late hour at which they returned to Marvin's and had their sex session, it was impractical for Omar to go home. He started sleeping over at Marvin's. "Escorts charge a lot more for overnight sessions, so how do I handle this?" Omar wanted to know.

"Isn't it better for you and your car to spend the night at Marvin's home?" I asked.

Omar lived with his mother in a one-bedroom apartment in a bad part of the Mission District. They had lived in the same apartment since 1985 and thus were protected by local rent-control regulations from the skyrocketing housing costs. Moving to another apartment in San Francisco was not an option for them. When Omar graduated from high school, his mother took on a second job to buy her son a brand-new car. Finding parking in his neighborhood was a terrible hassle and his car was vandalized repeatedly.

"Well, you're right about that. No, I won't charge Marvin. I believe that eventually he'll ask me to move in with him."

"Will you?"

"I'm thinking about that."

"That is very considerate of you!"

The affair with Marvin didn't stop Omar from seeing other clients. Before taking on sex work to help pay his student loan, Omar held a part-time waiter job and also played guitar. Still, he had always been short of funds. Now he earned serious money. He spent it as fast as it came in.

For many years, his mother had been working as a clerk at the Mission District Library, where her Spanish proved to be an asset. She had struggled financially to make ends meet and shelter her son from economic privation. Now it was Omar's turn to look after his mother. However much he complained about her, with his new income he wholeheartedly helped Dolores live better.

But at periodic intervals he would rant against sex work, blaming it for his diminished libido, especially with women. Like other sex workers, when he felt sorry for himself he raised his fee. Turning tricks for $80 was suddenly viewed as an imposition; at $100 they became more bearable; at $140 they were only a slight inconvenience.

Omar also worked briefly for an escort agency. This agency would not allow him to use his real name. He called himself Sabino after a Basque national hero. The agency listed him on its Web site as "Sabino, 22 y/o, very handsome Basque, total top, always in control." A client who had visited Bilbao told Omar that he didn't look the least bit Basque. As I had instructed him, Omar came up with an improvisation on the spur of the moment. "I am Sicilian on my father's side and Basque on my mother's." Anxious to be penetrated, the client did not pursue the subject.

Except for his mother, Omar told everyone that he was a hustler. This included his girlfriend, the men he was dating for free, his fellow students, and Marvin. The psychiatrist actually enjoyed hearing Omar's whoring tales. I believe that Omar was so open about this aspect of his life partially for the shock value. But even more so, because of his trauma in youth upon discovering his true ethnicity, Omar had developed a compulsion to be himself. I told him that not everyone needed to know his business, to which he replied, "You write books about hustlers and your personal experiences with them. What's the difference?"

"I am at the very end of my working career. You're at the beginning. One day you might apply for a teaching job and your hustling will be held against you." Omar agreed that I had a valid point but continued informing the world at large that he was a hustler.

While all of this was going on, Omar and I developed a special friendship. Sometimes the two of us hang out with Omar's gang, male as well as female. I have also introduced him to many of my friends. Most of them are instantly charmed by him. Some of my older friends have even grown jealous of me. How, they wonder, could I have become a *nonpaying* friend of such a handsome escort?

In celebration of their first anniversary, Marvin invited Omar to travel with him abroad.

"I told Marvin that we could leave only after the end of the school year," Omar said. "So he goes, 'You choose the country.' Without thinking, I say, 'Let's go to Morocco.' Marvin says 'OK, we'll travel there in July.'"

The trip to Morocco was a watershed for both men. The travel stress, the heat, and the Moroccan street urchins brought all of Marvin's sexual kinks out of the closet. Omar came face to face with his "homeland" and detested it.

Unfortunately, I heard only Omar's version of the trip. He hated the heat, the lack of hygiene, and, most of all, the pestering and jostling of the ubiquitous street vendors, guides, and beggars. He also did not care much for the food. Marvin, on the other hand, took an immediate liking to the architecture, the crafts in the bazaars, and the Moroccan men—especially the young guys in the streets. He was certain that they were flirting with him.

"In Rabat we had a serious fight," Omar said. "Marvin wanted sex constantly. He said the hot weather made him horny. It always happened when I was totally exhausted by the heat and depressed by the country. Marvin was so turned on by the Moroccans that he went out by himself to cruise. He found a guy who would do it with him for money, but I was in the hotel room. Where could he have taken him? One evening, when I refused to have sex with him, we had a big fight and almost terminated the trip and our relationship. Then, out of the blue, Marvin says, 'I want you to piss on me. I never had the nerve to tell you that I liked water sports.'

"At that moment, I was really in a mood to do just that to Marvin. He got so terribly excited by my pissing on him that I was afraid he would have a stroke. You know, he has high blood pressure. He doesn't take his meds like he should, because they make him impotent. So here we are in a fancy bathtub in our hotel, me pissing on Marvin while he sucks on my toes. Then he wanted me to smack his ass with my belt. After he came, I made him take a shower and then fucked him on the bed real hard. After Marvin climaxes, he doesn't like to get screwed because it's uncomfortable. I got off on hurting him and, like a true masochist, he enjoyed the pain. When I was done, we were good friends once again."

Omar and Marvin traveled by bus from Rabat to Casablanca and then flew to Tangier, Omar's birthplace. There, many of the natives still speak Spanish and Omar could have conversed in his native tongue. "My mother always made fun of the way Spanish was spoken in Tangier. I heard the natives through her ears and it made me cringe. I refused to speak in Spanish. This seemed strange to Marvin and even to myself. But that's the way I felt."

From Tangier they took the ferry to Algeciras, where Omar's mother hails from. "Did you speak Spanish there?" I asked Omar.

"Hardly. I was afraid that they would make fun of me because I was Moroccan. I spoke English everywhere."

"But you speak Spanish like your mother. Why would they make fun of you?"

"I don't know. Because of my skin. My mother fucked with my mind too much about Moroccans."

"Did anyone, anywhere, on this trip make fun of you?"

"No. They took both of us for Americans and wanted our dollars. We could have been extraterrestrials for all they cared."

Instead of returning to Morocco, Omar and Marvin flew to the island of Majorca. "There my Spanish came back to me. We spent five days lying on the beach. Every night, before going to bed, Marvin licked my feet while I pissed on him in the tub and whacked his ass with my belt. He was the happiest I had ever seen him. Truthfully, I was overjoyed to be out of Morocco. Unfortunately, we had to fly to Rabat to catch our flight back to San Francisco."

The trip altered the relationship between Marvin and Omar. The psychiatrist gave up any pretense of being Omar's mentor. He became his sex slave and, out of bed, his docile partner. Omar moved in with him. Because Marvin was so beholden to Omar sexually, he wanted them to become a real couple. He even suggested that they register at City Hall as domestic partners. Omar refused because he didn't consider himself Marvin's lover.

Until the trip to Morocco, Omar had been paid on a per-session basis (plus bonuses and incentives). Once he became Marvin's "sugar son," the psychiatrist bought him a new car and gave him an associate credit card in his own name. "And, you know," Omar concluded, "I still charge him one hundred dollars every time we have sex. I need to stop spending money all the time. Marvin is such a penny-pincher."

"Not a very successful pincher, if you ask me. Now that you live with Marvin, how does he cope with your screwing around with other men professionally and for free?"

"He doesn't care as long as we're together."

"Well, how long will that be?"

"I don't know. I'm all confused about where I came from, where my sexuality is taking me, what I'll do when I graduate, and what shape my life will take. Yes, I am a high-maintenance trophy boy. But don't worry; Marvin has enough money to take care of me. I am already in his will. People with high blood pressure who don't take their meds die young."

"Omar, older people are notoriously fickle. They keep changing their wills, disinheriting relatives, and even boyfriends who displease them for this or that reason. Don't count your—"

"Whose side are you on?"

"I have a conflict of interest. I am your mentor, and I'm duty-bound to look after your interests. But poor Marvin is setting himself up."

"Damn it, he's a brilliant, high-society psychiatrist. He knows what he is doing."

"Maybe his patients think so. But he certainly hasn't analyzed his relationship with you and is bound to be terribly disappointed sooner or later."

"Well, what do you expect? He's a masochist."

I visited Omar once while Marvin was out of town. He and Marvin live in a four-bedroom condo in Pacific Heights with a beautiful view of the bay. Omar refers to it as "our home." A few years earlier, Marvin adopted a cat from the SPCA. I have never found out her real name. Derisively, Omar calls her La Generala, Spanish for a general's wife. I have been around cats most of my life. La Generala is the most odious pet in my experience, and not only because she has a lousy personality. She is an enormously fat feline with khaki-colored fur and looks like an overgrown, army-issue cat. She hates Omar and all other strangers, viewing them as competitors for Marvin's attention. When I tried to pet her, she bit me hard enough to draw blood.

"Do you know why La Generala is such a fat cat?" Omar asked. "As soon as she starts her obnoxious meowing, Marvin gives her a can of soft food. That will shut her up for a few hours. Then she starts again and Marvin feeds her another can. He even gets up at night to keep her quiet. Maybe he didn't take Animal Psychology 101 when he was a student."

"If you hadn't told me that Marvin was a psychiatrist, I would've assumed that he also didn't take courses in human psychology."

"Why do you say that?"

"Don't you see that he handles you like he handles La Generala? He has made you into a fat cat."

"Because he's a masochist?"

"How would *I* know? Ask him; he's the psychiatrist."

Omar started his affair with Marvin as an escort—an independent contractor. Wittingly or otherwise, Marvin has become Omar's sugar daddy. As a rule in such relationships, the "son" thinks that his "daddy" does not bestow sufficient "sugar" on him. The daddy feels shortchanged because, invariably, the son does not give him enough sex and, to boot, doesn't show true filial gratitude.

In my opinion, a client who entices his sex worker to become a paid lover will come to regret it. A sex worker who assumes the role of a "sugar son" is setting himself up for constant bickering with his new daddy and, eventually, a nasty separation. I suspect that the more aggrieved party is likely to be the older man.

Chapter 11

Sex Work for Better Self-Esteem

Some five years ago I placed one of my frequent "Older Seeks Younger" ads in a San Francisco freebie paper. I inserted the ad in a mainly straight publication that features a "Man Seeking Man" section in its personals. Bisexuals and closeted gays can bring such publications to their workplaces or homes without giving away their secret.

Winston Lee responded to my ad by leaving a voice mail message. He said that he was nineteen years old and in his first year at City College. He added very quickly, "I'm Asian, smooth, five seven, one eighty-nine." Then he slowed down and gave a box number where I could write him and leave my phone number. Obviously, he did not want me to call him at home. I had to play back the message a number of times before deciphering his personal stats. Once I understood them, I knew why Winston had recorded part of it rapidly. He was a *heavy* guy trying to minimize the impact.

Most of my sex workers have been thin young men. As I wrote in *A Consumer's Guide to Male Hustlers,* a number of them bordered on anorexic. Actually, only a few really overweight sex workers ply their trade because of the prevailing prejudice in the gay community against "chubbies."[1] However, I happen not to mind heavy partners. Maybe I am a *latent* "chubby chaser."

Over the phone, Winston told me that he had had only one gay encounter in his life. He was eager to expand his horizons. "Are you sure that you're gay?" I asked.

"Of course I'm sure." He sounded almost annoyed with my question.

"There's a big age difference between us."

"I *know.* I answer your ad, don't I?"

He told me that he was an American-born Chinese studying marketing at City College and working part time for an upscale department store. Winston lived at home and had no car. We arranged a meeting place where I would pick him up. "What will you be wearing, Winston? I don't want to drive off with the wrong guy," I joked.

"A blue windbreaker and black pants. Don't worry, you'll recognize me."

Winston was right about being easily recognizable. He stood under a streetlight and I could see him clearly. Though framed by a double chin, his face was handsome. I thought he was almost cute. I believe not too many gays would use this adjective with such an overweight person.

At home, we had a long conversation. It turned out that we shared many interests. Winston was an affable person, as talkative as myself, and we took to each other right away. Unfortunately, in bed things did not work out as nicely. Winston was completely inexperienced in the art of lovemaking. He could not even breathe and kiss simultaneously. "Breathe through your nose and kiss with your mouth," I instructed him. But he could not coordinate the two activities. Much of the time, instead of kissing, he was gasping for air.

He thought that blowing me would be a simpler task. But like an inexperienced diver, he kept surfacing in panic, taking deep gulps of air. In agitation, he bit my dick. I decided to postpone our blowing session for another occasion.

One has to grade the performance of free sexual partners on a different scale than those of professional escorts. Even so, Winston received a failing grade. The only remarkable thing about Winston's sexual performance was his ejaculation. It was as impressive as that of porn stars—and their climaxes are enhanced by the film editor.

When we were done, I wondered whether we should meet again. I liked Winston a lot as a person, but he was a terrible sex partner. I was sure that with patience and perseverance I could teach him to become a good kisser and maybe even to give passable blow jobs. Still, I asked myself whether it would be it worth the effort. In the end, the issue became moot. Winston didn't give me his phone number and never called back.

* * *

Four years later, I saw an ad on the Internet by a twenty-three-year-old Asian student seeking "a generous older man for good times." His screen name was "yng4oldrgnt." A promising ad, I thought to myself, and sent him an e-mail. He answered my message, giving me his stats: "Asian, 23 y/o, 5' 7", 194." He added a postscript: "If you are OK with me being somewhat heavy, please let me know and I'll send you my *pic*." He signed with the initial "W".

I thought that "somewhat heavy" didn't do justice to the advertiser's weight, but this wasn't a problem as far as I was concerned. In our following transmissions we exchanged photos. When I opened his e-mail attachment, I saw the face of Winston Lee, four years older. I sent him my phone number and he got in touch with me the next evening. "Why didn't you ever call me after our first meeting?" I asked.

"I think you're disappointed because I don't know how to kiss and suck. Guess what?"

"You went to kissing and sucking school and graduated with honors?"

"I still don't know how to kiss or suck."

"But, Winston, this time around it's serious. You advertise as a professional escort. A dissatisfied client might report you to—to the Better Business Bureau!"

"Very funny. To be honest with you, I already have a client and get canned because I don't have enough sex experience."

We chatted some more. The more we spoke, the more we clicked. Four years earlier it seemed to me that Winston had a very heavy schedule. Now he held two part-time jobs and carried twelve credits at San Francisco State. I suspected that he was a bit of a workaholic.

Lacking basic lovemaking skills, Winston did not deserve to be paid for escorting. However, I still believed that I could tutor him. After his apprenticeship, we would enjoy each other's company *and* have good sex. It was worth a try.

"I already have a regular escort. But I need a relief worker. My regular, Michael, is going to Los Angeles next week. If things work out between us, we'll get together every three days for the next two weeks. After Michael returns, once a week or so. Even though you aren't professional yet, I'll pay you the same as I do Michael, fifty dollars per session. It isn't much, but it's steady work."

Winston agreed, and we set up a date.

Though grossly "overnourished," Winston looked well—better than four years earlier. I served him tea and we chatted. Like Lloyd, he used only the present tense when he spoke, which was confusing at times. He had a pleasant voice that compensated for his odd grammar.

As overweight people often do, he assured me that his present poundage was a fleeting episode. "I'm a teeny bit heavier than I am last time. You know, I lose weight in my early twenties when I exercise a lot. But then I get so busy with school and work and stuff that I regain all of it. Since I meet you the first time, I haven't date much. I'm waiting until I lose weight again. I take care of it as soon as the semester is over. The doctor say my cholesterol is too high. I have to lose a few pounds."

"In the meantime, while you're not dating, you hustle?"

"It is just something new to try out."

"Well, then, let's see how you perform as an escort."

Though Winston had gained weight since our last meeting, he still had a fairly firm body rather than mounds of jellied fat. Learning how to kiss and blow properly did not come easily to him. It took some ten sessions before he became proficient in these skills. This was a terrific deal for him: He got paid while learning his craft!

Once he felt more sure of himself, he even came up with a unique technique. He would use the considerable weight of his head and, with his chin, massage my upper back between my shoulder blades. He could do this for the longest time. Since this is the area in which my tension resides, it was a most relaxing sensation. I tried to reciprocate, but I lacked Winston's stamina, and the weight of my chin was negligible compared to his.

It didn't take many meetings to establish a true camaraderie between us. Our personalities complemented each other. Winston likes older men; I enjoy the company of younger guys. Winston has poor learning skills; I have been a teacher much of my life. In general, I am a poor shopper. Winston knows all about buying and selling. I have to struggle with my computers; Winston makes love to them. As a matter of fact, the first time he visited me in his new sex worker capacity, I was in the throes of a computer crisis. He solved it in minutes.

Winston had relatively few expenses because he lived with his parents. He had income from a number of sources. In addition to his job at the department store—where he had worked when we first met—he sold collectors' comic books on the Internet. He had taken out a student loan. During my time with him, he made a tidy bundle trading shares wildly on the NASDAQ. It was obvious to me that Winston had no urgent financial need to do sex work. Paradoxically, it was equally obvious that we would not see each other on a regular basis without the fifty-dollar "honorarium." Certainly, my contribution was a welcome addition, especially since Winston kept buying new gadgets as soon as they were invented. But he would have survived quite well without my help.

My payments served a different purpose in Winston's life. They enhanced his self-image, and he needed the boost.[2] In many respects, he was a somewhat insecure person. For instance, he worried about his poor language skills. Even though he was born in San Francisco, his first language had been Cantonese. As an adult, he still had a poor grasp of English grammar. His instructors at San Francisco State were confused by his strange sentence structure. Until I came upon the scene, he received Cs or below on his term papers.

But his principal insecurity was weight related. Because he was exclusively attracted to older men, he must have wondered whether these gentlemen were interested in him only because he made himself available to them. Maybe a *chubby* young guy such as Winston was the best they could do. Every time I handed him his "honorarium," it assured him that he was truly desirable.

Winston was a busy beaver handicapped by poor time management. In addition to his various jobs, he liked to hang out with his friends. His hectic schedule resulted in sleep deprivation. Eventually, his body forced him to cut classes, stop working for a day, and catch up on his sleep. He made time for our sex sessions because, after all, they were a paying job and he was a workaholic. He was not a particularly lustful person, but I believe that Winston enjoyed our "sexcapades." Certainly, his enormous ejaculations could not have been a sham. But I doubt that he would have freed his schedule on a regular basis for nonpaying trysts.

Winston allowed plenty of time for our sessions. He used public transportation to get to my home, which made the sessions even more time-consuming. On numerous occasions, as soon as he arrived, usually at 8:00 p.m., he would call one of his friends and ask to be picked up at 11:00. We followed a fixed routine. After chatting briefly, Winston would present various school projects which required my help. Once I took care of Winston's schoolwork, we would move from the living room into my study. There Winston would sit in front of the computer monitor, straightening out the messes I had made since our last session. He hated reading and tried to do as little of it as possible. But on-screen instructions were holy. He studied text on the monitor with lawyerly attention, and whatever work he did on the computer was faultless.

I believe that Winston wanted—needed—social interaction with an older man even more than physical contact. Only after finishing our various tasks did we get to the carnal part. In bed, we behaved like old lovers. Our sex was comforting rather than thrilling. This was agreeable to me. I regarded Winston as a close friend with whom I also happened to have a sex-buddy relationship.

Winston went shopping with me on a number of occasions. On these excursions he served as my consultant. However, he regarded himself as my little helper. (Well, maybe as my *big* helper.) When I bought a television, he insisted on carrying the bulky package to my car.

Winston's graduation was scheduled at the end of the 2000 spring term. His final courses were difficult and all of them required term papers. Usually, he finished writing them the night before they were due. I would proof them (via e-mail) in the wee hours of the morning. In the meantime, Winston started interviewing for a full-time job. I helped with his résumé and cover letters.

Two weeks before the term was over, Winston was invited to an interview with a leading toy store for a management-trainee position. He had enough sales experience under his belt and, with his college degree, had excellent qualifications. When we got together a few days before the interview, I polished his résumé and conducted a mock interview to prepare him for the real thing. Three days later, he called to tell me that he had been offered the position. "And, Joseph, I'm taking you out for lunch. How about next week on Monday?"

Winston knew a lot about restaurants. He chose a fancy place with excellent food. During our lunch, he had a sad story to tell me. He had miscalculated his graduation date. It turned out he was six credits shy of his bachelor's degree. He would take two courses in the fall semester and graduate the following year.

"This means that you won't have much time to visit with me when you start your classes again," I observed.

"I'll always make time for you, Joseph. You know that."

"Well, we'll stay friends; that's for sure. We can go out or—" Then I realized that his summer would be relatively free. "We don't need to worry about this until the fall. You'll have plenty of time after work during the summer."

"Sure. Send me an e-mail with a good time for you."

Over the next few weeks, we exchanged a number of e-mails. Winston's jobs were working out fine; he had bought a digital camera and was busy trying it out; he went to Las Vegas for a weekend; we would see each other soon. Then, after a long silence, a good-bye note. The message was titled "You won't see me anytime soon." Winston would be busy the rest of the summer.

Usually, once my sex workers stop escorting me, the relationship is over. (The two notable exceptions are Beauregard and Omar, whom I have written about earlier.) I believe that the reason for this is contextual—that is, the sex work is an integral part of our interaction. When this part is removed, the relationship collapses.

As an independent contractor, Winston was entitled to bring our working (and social) relationship to an abrupt end. Had he and I been strictly friends, I would have pursued the matter. "Have I done something to offend you?" I would have asked him. As a friend, an explanation would have been in order. As a sex worker, he didn't owe me anything. I assume that he took me out for lunch to acknowledge my help with his résumé.

I am always saddened when I do not get feedback in situations such as this. I believe one can improve behavior only by learning from mistakes. I would have liked to know what went wrong between us. But, then, nothing at all may have gone wrong. By being my sex worker for a year and a half, Winston improved his self-image, learned basic lovemaking skills, and made a bit of extra money. Then it was time for him to move on with his life.

When planning this book, it was not been my intention to write a memoir titled *A Client in Search of an Escort*. But it has turned out that way due to my quest for Winston's substitute. In a way, I am pleased with this unexpected development. I do not want readers to assume that using the sex workers' services regularly and *meaningfully* requires only phoning them to set up dates. As with any worthwhile endeavor, ups and downs occur; uneventful times are followed by crises; and unexpected developments happen.

My affair with Winston came close to resembling a boyfriend relationship. When it was over, I was hurt and confused. But I had no time to brood or feel sorry for myself. My immediate assignment was to recruit a new sex worker to fill the vacant position.

Chapter 12

"Mature" Sex Workers

The phenomenon of older sex workers (roughly, those over thirty years old) still plying their trade is relatively new. It started in the United States (and probably other countries) in the latter part of the twentieth century. Until then, practically all sex workers were in the streets or in bars and were younger men.

Then the gay press (and gay-friendly publications) came into being the 1960s.[1] Very early in the game, they opened their pages to gay personal and business advertisements. Pretty soon, their escort columns became a never-never land. Men who would not have dreamed of prostituting themselves on the streets or in bars were willing to advertise their services in gay publications. Advertising for clients in print was much more discreet than trying to snare them in the streets.

Some of these men were older guys who, often misguidedly, believed that they looked much younger than their chronological age. They shed as many years off their ages as they thought they could get away with in their ads and competed with much younger sex workers. Since respondents to sex workers' ads would see the advertisers only when they arrived at their homes (or wherever they met), the older escorts did not need to worry about their more youthful competitors. On the street, clients eyeball workers. In plain sight of most buyers, a forty-four-year-old sex worker cannot compete successfully against a man half his age. But standing on the client's threshold, a forty-four-year-old posing as a man of thirty has no competition. Certainly, the client can turn him away. But no guarantee exists that when another escort arrives, he won't be as old, or even older.

Over the years, two things happened. First, workers' lies about their age became more and more egregious. Second, it gradually became more acceptable to see older men advertising their services as sex workers. I believe that this upward shift has *benefited* clients. I will discuss this point more fully at the end of the chapter. However, as I have already noted, the deceitfulness of the vast majority of advertisers about their age may disqualify them from calling themselves sex workers rather than hustlers.

* * *

Some time ago, I saw a massage ad in a local paper. It read:

Release Massage
by cute, smooth, trim, 36, Native American/Jewish finger wizard.

At the time, I had two regular sex workers and, in any case, release massages are not of great interest to me. But the Native American/Jewish combination was irresistible. I have always been inordinately attracted to Native Americans but have had only a few partners from this ethnic group. I had never been intimate with a man who was half Native American and half Jewish. I gave my regulars a break and called the "finger wizard" for an appointment. He spoke in a sexy, resonant baritone voice. We made a date for the following day. He charged sixty dollars for his massage. His name was Edmond.

Edmond arrived right on time, driving a 1998 Taurus. His facial features were a subtle blend of his ethnic heritage. His straight, jet-black hair was long, almost reaching to his shoulders. He had a handsome, intriguing face, but not that of a thirty-six-year-old man. If I judged correctly, he was pushing fifty! When he described himself on the phone, he told me his height and weight. Although I couldn't recall precisely what he had said, I was sure from the stats he had provided that he was height-weight proportionate. Had this not been the case, I would have made a mental note of it. The Edmond I saw in front of me needed to go on a diet.

I asked Edmond to take a seat in my living room and offered him juice and cookies. All of my Native American partners had been shy, bordering on taciturn. In contrast, Edmond was a great conversationalist. Without prompting, he told me that he had a full-time job as a paralegal, and that this was his second time hustling (his word!). "The first time was when my lover and I broke up, ten years ago. Now that I'm older, I just give sexual massages."

He spoke a bit about his experiences as a masseur. Abruptly, he stopped. "I'm probably yakking too much. Why would you care?"

"It might interest you, Edmond, that not long ago my book, *A Consumer's Guide to Male Hustlers,* was published. In it, I wrote a lot about masseurs." I showed him the book cover.

"So *you* are the author? I own your book."

"Well, what do you think of it?"

"I enjoyed reading it. You write that hustlers fib about their age. Can you guess how old I really am?"

"I'm not good at guessing ages. How old are you?"

"Forty-six. But everybody thinks I look much, much younger."

"Everybody" did not include me. "Tell me about your ethnic mix," I said.

"Well, I'm the son of a Navajo woman from Window Rock, Arizona. My Jewish father lived all his life in Albuquerque. That's where my parents made their home. I had a lot of problems when I was in grade school because Indian children were not supposed to mix with Caucasians, and my parents had placed me in an all-white school. Finally, they sent me to boarding schools. I got an excellent education but didn't have a happy childhood. These schools were also a good training ground for homosexuality." Then, with a dismissive, deliberately limp-wristed gesture, he added, "Not that I needed much training."

The first time around, I try not to chitchat too much with my workers. I don't want an abbreviated sex session, and I also don't want them to feel that I monopolize their time. If they feel the urge to chat, we can do it after sex. With this in mind, I guided Edmond to my dedicated sex room.

Once Edmond took off his clothes, it became obvious that he was anything but smooth. He must have shaved his chest and arms a week earlier, but the hair had resprouted. As I had suspected, he easily could have lost twenty pounds and still not have been too thin. But he was a competent masseur. He used his body weight to great advantage when massaging my back. Subtly, his touch conveyed to me that he was attracted to me sexually. I became even more aware of it when he sat on the small of my back and I felt his hardness. Surprisingly, he told me to turn over before massaging my arms or legs. He was too experienced a masseur to forget such details.

Lying face up, with Edmond straddling my body, I saw the lust in his eyes. His fully erect, long, thin circumcised cock was shaped like a scimitar. Suddenly, we were kissing. I don't recall who initiated our kissing; it just happened. The massage session was over and done with. We were making out passionately. Time passed. Softly, Edmond whispered in my ear, "I'll be back in a moment."

I assumed he was going to use the bathroom. But he was doing something in the living room, where he had left his clothes. A moment later he was back. In his right hand he held a condom and a small bottle of lubricant. "I want you to fuck me, Joseph," he said. The higher pitch of his voice indicated his extreme arousal.

Under the rules of the engagement, the client tells the sex worker what *he* wishes to do or to be done. Screwing Edmond had not been on my agenda. But at this stage we had stopped being worker and client. We were sex partners, and Edmond had an equal say in choreographing the session. "OK," I mused to myself, "I'll rise to the occasion!"

Edmond was a superb bottom. We climaxed simultaneously. He didn't even touch himself to achieve orgasm. Spent, we lay in each other's embrace. "I'm a slut, aren't I?" he asked languidly.

"In your line of work, being sluttish is an advantage. By the way, why do you state in your ad that you are smooth?"

"Aren't Indians supposed to be smooth? I shave my chest, don't I?"

"The Great Spirit created Native Americans with smooth skin. Your Creator made you hairy. Therefore, I would suggest that you don't describe yourself as 'smooth' in your ad. If asked, tell your clients that you shave your body."

It turned out that Edmond was a political person, involved with many groups: Native Americans, gay Native Americans, Jews of color, radical fairies; the list went on and on. "I'm still in the closet about being a sex worker, though my friends have started to suspect."

"You aren't really doing it for the money, are you?"

"No, for the hell of it. But, you know, the money is nice."

Eventually, Edmond went in the bathroom to take a shower. I got up and put the sixty dollars near his clothes. I was debating with myself whether I would make future appointments with Edmond. As previously stated, johns who stiff their clients almost always justify it by saying, "He [the sex worker] enjoyed it as much as I did. Why should I pay him?" Now *I* was thinking this way about Edmond. "In the future we should do it for free! We'll *both* have a ball." Of course,

I knew from long experience that this would never happen. Sex workers may give it for free to some and charge others. But normally, they don't let the same person have sex for free once he has paid for it, however much they have enjoyed it.

I was mulling over in my own mind why I was reluctant to engage Edmond for future sessions after his splendid performance. "He is fat and hairy and old," I said to myself. "And a very good lay," I added, to be fair to him. Winston too is fat—far fatter than Edmond—and was initially a poor lay. So why didn't I mind paying Winston? Maybe because Winston had made full disclosure *before* arriving at my home as a sex worker. He told me his true weight and warned me that he was inexperienced. In contrast, Edmond had misrepresented himself completely. Again, to be fair, had he told me his real age and weight, I might never have invited him.

While I was still pondering all of this, Edmond emerged from the bathroom in his underwear, his potbelly showing. He put on his pants. Out of his the right pocket he took a large comb and passed it through his hair. I was standing and he was sitting, giving me a good view of the crown of his head. As he tilted his head forward to comb out his long hair, I saw the roots. They were prematurely white! On second thought, maybe they were *maturely* white. For all I knew, Edmond was *fifty*-six years old or even older. When he raised his head, he noticed my startled look and must have understood the reason. "My cosmetologist is on vacation," he said apologetically.

I came close to blurting out, "Don't ever go on assignment when your cosmetologist is taking a holiday." As far as I was concerned, the matter was closed. No more appointments with Edmond.

* * *

My experience with Edmond notwithstanding, mature sex workers present a number of advantages to their clients. First, they are usually more experienced than their younger colleagues. Second, and more important, they tend to have a much better attitude toward their vocation. As I have already written, young sex workers often feel sorry for themselves. In contrast, much older workers are inordinately proud that they can still command a fee for their services and fool clients about their age. Third, they are much more likely than younger workers to think in a businesslike manner.

The first point, that older workers have more experience, is self-explanatory. But two last points need further elaboration. Older workers usually have a better attitude. Edmond must have known for many years that he was a wanton man. Happily, he has learned to channel his sluttish energy into dollar production. The much younger author Rick Whitaker, mentioned in Chapter 3, has a similar disposition.[2] He too harnesses it into a moneymaking machine. But Rick is unhappy. He can clearly hear society's censorious voice demanding of him, "With your great talents, all you can do is prostitute yourself?" To this question he has no good answer and hangs his head in shame.

But at forty-six, it is to Edmond's credit that clients are still willing to pay him for his less-than-perfect body, and in spite of his hoary hair. Young Rick despises the gentlemen who compensate him so generously for his begrudgingly offered sexual services. Edmond, on the other hand, rejoices that his clients believe—or pretend—that he is a young, debonair escort.

Here is an illustration of my third point, that of a businesslike attitude. Through *A Consumer's Guide* I got to know, on a *social* basis, sex worker Misha. Born in Minsk, which was part of the USSR when his parents moved to this country, he has done well for himself in a capitalist environment. At the age of forty-five he gave up his job as a city employee and became a full-time, successful sex worker. We have become good friends and lunch together frequently. Presently, Misha is forty-eight years old, but his ad reads: "Yuri, good-looking, tall and muscular Russian, 36 y/o, $100 in, $125 out." Over lunch he told me the following story.

One day, a married man called him about the ad. He proposed visiting him once a week before going to his regular job, between 6:00 and 6:30 in the morning. He offered forty dollars for a weekly, early-morning quickie.

"I told the caller," Misha said, "that I wanted to think this over and asked him to call me again the next day. On the one hand, it was an insulting offer. Less than half of what I usually charge. On the other hand, hotels also reduce their room price by half or even more if they haven't rented out a unit by late afternoon. Early morning is my 'downtime.' Any money I can make then is better than none. The guy would stay for only thirty minutes and all he wants is a hand job."

"Did you see the client?"

"Yes, once. He never called again. I suppose he wanted a one-time bargain, or maybe he didn't care for me. It doesn't matter. I learned a lesson."

"What was the lesson?"

"Maximizing my *total* income."

As a matter of fact, most older masseurs and escorts reduce their fees once they admit to forty years of age or so. This certainly makes at least some workers more affordable to the general public.

Young sex workers often get into male prostitution through a series of coincidences over which they had little control. They have grave doubts about the validity of their escort work and usually have no insights about male prostitution that they can share with their clients. In contrast, sex work does not just happen to older men. Becoming escorts is a conscious, carefully planned decision on their part.

In an article titled "Sex Work As Health Care: Confessions of a 'Pleasure Activist,'" Don Shewey states: "I came into this line of work at the advanced age of 39."[3] Shewey writes that he "heals through pleasure" and, as *part* of the healing, he has engaged with clients in a number of sexual activities described in one long paragraph. I am certain that if a client can ignore the age issue, he will get better value for his money (sensually, intellectually, and even spiritually) from the long-in-the-tooth healer than from the hunkiest nineteen-year-old.

I have come full circle. I started this chapter with a tale of good sex provided by an older worker who lied about his age. I wrote that, confronted with the worker's real age, I felt cheated. I speculated that had I been told the worker's accurate stats on the phone, I would not have hired him in the first place. But later on in the chapter I write that older sex workers benefit their clients. So what *am* I saying?

Here is what I would have suggested to Edmond had he asked for my advice. First, he should advertise his services as a bottom, not as a masseur. Fewer bottom ads are placed in the paper and therefore far less competition exists. Second, he should advertise his real age and tell callers his real weight, if asked. Third, instead of charging sixty dollars for a massage—the going rate—he should ask for the same amount, but as a bottom sex worker. This rate would be one half or less what the younger bottoms receive. A potential client would then be in a position to make an intelligent decision based on full disclosure.

I believe that some clients would be willing to hire Edmond as a low-budget bottom escort. Knowing his *real* age, they would marvel at how good he is rather than be angry about his deceitfulness. With his hair dyed properly, Edmond would avoid accentuating his age.

Edmond's age became an issue for me because he made it into one. Had I chosen Edmond *in spite* of his "maturity" (for his interesting ethnic mix and his lower fee as an *escort*), I would have enjoyed my session with him, and not only physically. Moreover, unlike Michael, he would have been my intellectual equal.

Following is one example of a truthful older sex worker apparently doing well for himself. In *A Consumer's Guide* (p. 16), I cited the following ad to demonstrate that older men are, indeed, engaged in sex work, though at a reduced price.

Naked Runner, 51 y/o, $40

Three years later, the runner's chronologically updated ad is still . . . running. Now it reads:

Naked runner . . . 54 y/o. Big balls. $50 out.[4]

Chapter 13

Seven Guidelines

I believe that my success with sex workers is unique neither to me nor to San Francisco escorts. I am sure that other gay men all over the world have similar success stories to relate.

In November 1986, I traveled from San Francisco to Zurich to testify at a court hearing. The affair would take only one day of consultations with my lawyer and one morning of testimony. But it was essential that I be well rested and over any jet lag before the court hearing. To recharge my batteries after the long flight from California, I chose to begin my trip by spending three days in Barcelona. From previous experience, I knew that I would have more fun there than in Zurich. I decided to arrive in Barcelona on a Saturday evening and leave for Zurich the following Tuesday.

At 2:00 in the afternoon on Sunday, I went to a large Barcelona bathhouse. It was almost full, but luckily I managed to get a private room. It seemed that everyone but me was having a good time. In *A Consumer's Guide to Male Hustlers* (pp. 75-77), I made a point of how psychologically devastating it can be to be rejected over and over again in a brief period of time. Luckily, in the Barcelona bathhouse I did not have to suffer rejection. Many sex workers were on duty. I spoke to most of them but waited patiently for a partner who wouldn't charge me. After all, I had all the time in the world. Any minute now, a knight in shining armor—more correctly described, with a towel draped around his waist—would present himself, asking permission to join me in my cubicle.

Having been duly rejected by the few nonsex workers to whom I was attracted, I posted myself near the entrance door, waiting for new arrivals. A long line was present in front of the cashier's cage, which was located inside the bathhouse. From my vantage point, I could clearly see a young guy with long blond hair and pretty blue eyes waiting for his turn to gain admission. He was obviously not a local.

When he reached the cage, he said in German, "Before I pay to get in, will you tell me how warm it is inside the sauna? I mean, how many degrees?" The cashier did not understand German. The guy repeated the question slowly but in a much louder voice.

I am usually not attracted to fair men with blond hair and blue eyes, such as the German guy. But him I liked. I walked over to the cashier's desk. "I speak German," I said to the new arrival. "May I translate for you?"

"But this is *wunderbar!* Please ask—"

"I know what your question was. I'll ask the cashier."

Once the cashier understood the question he gave me a strange look. "How the hell am I supposed to know how many *degrees* the sauna is? Tell this *caballero* that he's holding up the line."

I translated the answer, and added, "Why don't you come in? The sauna's pretty warm."

"Are you certain?"

"Yes."

He paid for a locker and was admitted into the bathhouse. He really did have beautiful eyes. With his compact swimmer's body, he was sort of cute. Playing the role of host, I escorted him to the locker room. On the way, I showed him the sauna, the steam room, and the showers. I decided to keep a close watch on him so I wouldn't lose him in the crowd. He changed, showered, and then entered the sauna. I suspected that he would take his time savoring its warmth. I had learned only two things about him: his name was Helmut, and he was from Frankfurt.

While waiting for Helmut to emerge from the sauna, I had to deal with my pangs of conscience. I had not been forthright with him. I do not particularly like saunas. I had spent only a few moments in the Barcelona sauna and had no idea whether it would be warm enough for finicky patrons such as Helmut. But I wanted him to stay in the bathhouse. In my mind was an open and a hidden agenda. The open agenda was to lure him to my lair. The bait would be that we could converse there in his language. But this was a long shot. Even without Spanish, Helmut could and would find younger and more handsome suitors.

My hidden agenda was more devious. I have known German since childhood but had not spoken it for a very long time. I needed to practice this language before my court appearance. By rights, I should have flown directly to Zurich and practiced my German there. Instead, I was blabbing in Spanish with bathhouse hustlers. I hoped that I would be able to engage Helmut in a long conversation. We could discuss sauna temperatures in Barcelona as compared to Frankfurt or any other important topics he wanted to share with me.

Helmut was out of the sauna almost immediately, and he was upset. "Not warm enough!" he exclaimed. "Not warm at all. Almost frigid. Now what *shall* I do?" His forehead was wrinkled with a deep worry frown.

He looked so forlorn encountering a frigid sauna in a strange land that I was about to say, "Helmut, don't do anything rash. You're young, and you still have a lot to live for." Instead, I suggested, "May I invite you to my room?"

"What for?"

"Well, to talk and . . . whatever else happens between us."

His blue bedroom eyes gave me a long, probing look and then he said, "Well, there's a little complication."

"Complication?"

"Well, as you can see, I'm still young. I'm only twenty-one years old." He paused.

After a long silence, I felt it was my turn to say something. "Youth is a wonderful time of life," I assured him.

"For a young man, I've done a lot of traveling. Do you know that I've traveled as far as India?" Again he paused.

"I've been to India. Youth is a good time for traveling."

"*Generous* gentlemen in Germany and in other countries have helped me with my . . . traveling expenses." He stopped.

So this was the way the wind was blowing! "Would you allow me, Helmut, to be another such gentleman?"

"Yes, of course."

"Then maybe it would be proper for you to tell me the amount of the contribution I would be required to make." Linguistic circumlocutions sound much better in German than in English.

I could see that Helmut was doing sums in his mind. He had to convert German marks into Spanish pesetas. "Would twenty-five hundred pesetas be agreeable to you?" he asked.

Here I had an advantage over Helmut. I wasn't yet used to the new currency, and neither was he. But I had already received numerous quotes from sex workers ranging from 4,000 to 5,500 pesetas. For the larger figure, the worker would permit a *jodida,* penetration. Since I had no intention of screwing Helmut, I said, "Actually, I'll be happy to help you with four thousand pesetas." (At the time, the equivalent of about thirty dollars.)

"*Wunderbar,*" Helmut exclaimed. I was happy to see his frown turn into a faint smile. In the end, maybe I would make him forget the trauma of the underheated sauna, for which I bore some responsibility.

"Are you staying at a hotel here in Barcelona?"

"Yes."

"Can we go there? I *hate* it here."

"Of course we can go to my hotel. In fact, I would prefer that."

I complain incessantly that sex workers overcharge for their services. So why did I offer Helmut more than he had asked for?

With my long-term sex workers, I request and receive a preferred-client discount. The first time around, I negotiate the worker's fee based on the prevailing market price. Actually, I am wary of workers who initially charge considerably less than the going rate. (Just as I would question why a roofer underbids his competitors by a few thousand dollars.) Helmut was entitled to fair compensation. He had made an honest mistake, and I adjusted his fee.

My hotel was a short walk from the bathhouse. Helmut and I made small talk on our way. Suddenly, he stopped in front of a shoe store. Once again, he frowned deeply. Pointing to the display window, he asked, "Tell me, do you see what I see?"

"All I see are shoes. It *is* a shoe store. Are the shoe stores in Frankfurt different?"

"You really don't see?"

"Yes. I mean, no. What's so remarkable about this store?"

"But the display is *terrible*. It's a *disgrace*."

"Helmut, the store is closed because it's Sunday. Otherwise, I would be happy to translate for you while you explain all of this to the owner. Let's go."

Distracted by my hidden agenda at the bathhouse—conversing in German—I had neglected to discuss the on-the-bed agenda. What would Helmut be willing to perform in bed in exchange for the 4,000 pesetas? Sadly, it turned out that Helmut was unwilling to kiss at all.

However, in all other respects, he was a good enough worker. After the sex, Helmut and I conversed leisurely in German—not very profoundly, but enough to remove some of my rustiness in that language.

By the time we were ready to get dressed it was 6:00. "In Spain, people dine very late, Helmut. But I'm hungry. Maybe we can find a restaurant that will serve us something small, like a bowl of soup or a sandwich. May I invite you to join me?"

"Oh, this would be *wunderbar.* Later on, I'll go to a hustler bar where I can earn some more money. But it's much too early for that now. By all means, let's have a bite."

My encounter with Helmut, which started in the early afternoon, ended around 8:00 p.m. For 4,000 pesetas, I had an adequate sexual experience, socialized with the worker, and was intellectually stimulated by him (honing my German language skills).

Professional sex workers would decry Helmut's acceptance of my dinner invitation without compensation for his time. After all, he "escorted" me to the restaurant and kept me company. But I believe that both of us came out ahead. Unlike Helmut, who did not speak Spanish, I could have ordered a meal from room service and entertained myself watching television. Then I could have taken in a movie. Helmut was my guest for dinner, could talk to me in his language, and kept himself amused while waiting for his "shift" at the hustler bar. As for me, I have dined with more stimulating companions than Helmut. However, the greatest benefit was conversing in German. At the end of the evening both of us had enjoyed ourselves. It was *virtually* a date with a friend, including sex.

Some readers may dismiss this story as exceptional: too many coincidences turn out to be equally advantageous for both parties. With these skeptics in mind, I'll tell the story of my subsequent visit to the same bathhouse, one day later.

* * *

Only a few patrons were at the bathhouse on Monday in the early afternoon. It would have been better had I gone at nighttime, but I had to be at the airport at 6:00 the next morning to catch the flight to Zurich. However, all was not lost. There were three sex workers on duty.

After assuring myself that no free partners were available, I interviewed the three workers. I chose the least handsome of the bunch. The reason? He liked older men—he lived with a fifty-five-year-old judge—and he loved to talk. I had nothing but time on my hands and was in a mood to have sex and gab. His name was José, he was twenty-two years old, short, and a bit husky with dark eyes. He assured me that he liked kissing. José charged 5,000 pesetas.

Once we were in my cubicle, he said, "Today is my day off. My lover doesn't expect me to be home until very late."

"Does he know that you're cuckolding him?" I shaped the index and middle fingers of my right hand into a "V" sign and held them behind my head.

José laughed. "He's a judge, you know. He probably suspects. But this is my way of earning extra money."

We made love and we talked. Then we talked some more and made love again. I climaxed twice, and José once. Suddenly, I was overcome by "the sleepies." Too much sex? The remnants of jet lag? All I knew was that I needed to rest for a while. "José, please excuse me, but I must take a brief siesta. I'm fading fast."

"Do you mind if I take a siesta with you? I don't have a room, and I'm going to be at the bath for many hours."

In *A Consumer's Guide* I point out that it is not a good idea to fall asleep with complete *strangers* (regardless whether they are sex workers or just casual partners). José, even though a judge's protégé, could help himself to my clothes or shoes. How would I return to my hotel shoeless and without trousers? There was nothing else to steal in the room. All my valuables were locked in the bathhouse's safe-deposit box. It was a judgment call on my part. My clothes were not fancy, and José did not strike me as the type of young man who would pilfer from a client.

"OK, José, rest here with me." I handed him his fee. I did not want him to worry about it.

Both of us woke up at the same time. I felt refreshed and energetic. Psychologically, the little siesta with José, just like my dinner with Helmut, made the encounter less of a commercial transaction and more of a social event. "May I treat you to a cup of coffee?"

"Certainly."

At the snack bar, José asked whether he could also order a piece of cake. "Go ahead," I said. "I'll have a piece as well."

Before depositing my valuables, I had kept 5,500 pesetas in case I needed money to hire a sex worker. The 500 remaining pesetas were not enough to cover our order. I was embarrassed. "I'll have to go to my box and get some money."

"Permit me," José said, and paid the bill in full.

* * *

At a recent reading, I was asked whether I *liked* paying for sex. My answer was, "No, I would prefer to get it for free. But I'm glad that paying for it is an option." From long experience I know that in a bathhouse, given enough time and patience, one will always find a sex partner. But, most of the time, this partner of last resort is a man, as Beauregard used to say, whose dogs I would not allow to run with my dogs. (I am not putting down this imagined partner; if he had the choice, he too would not allow *his* dogs to run with mine!)

In Barcelona, had I waited until I found the partner of last resort, I would have returned to my hotel angry at myself for having wasted so much time for such minimal pleasure. It would have damaged my self-esteem, proving that the best I could do for myself was to have sex with a man I did not care for in the least. By paying for sex two days in a row, I assured myself that both experiences were physically and psychologically satisfying.

The satisfaction was enhanced by adding social components to the sexual experiences. This benefited not only me but my partners as well. These were not scripted events, but rather spontaneous happenings. The point is that I was open to them. Whimsical Helmut wanted to get out of the bathhouse as soon as he arrived. Most potential clients would have refused to indulge his whim. Why waste the price of admission to the bathhouse to humor capricious Helmut? Not every man would have been willing to take a siesta with a bathhouse hustler. An element of risk *was* involved.

I have just finished reading Aaron Lawrence's *The Male Escort's Handbook.*[1] I enjoyed the book thoroughly. I also had the pleasure of meeting Aaron in person twice at readings he gave in San Francisco. He is a charming man and a witty speaker. Surprisingly, although Aaron writes from an escort's point of view and I speak for the client, we make similar observations and agree on many issues. Aaron's approach to escorting is ethical, even compassionate, and always respectful of the client.

To my knowledge, he is the first writer to discuss a code of ethics for sex workers. ("As a sex worker you have an ethical obligation to do no harm to the client."[2]) An escort following his precepts would turn out to be a competent and responsible worker.[3]

The foundations of my knowledge of sex work go back to regular meetings with street hustlers in 1964. Reading Aaron's book afforded me an opportunity to check my old-fashioned approach against the postmodern, twenty-*first* century style of professional escorting. When I reached Chapter 19 ("Managing Your Money") my heart sank. My sex workers are nobodies compared to Aaron's cadre! Momentarily, I felt that I had no business at all writing about the subject. The new generation of workers for whom Aaron wrote his manual are in a *much* more advanced league and play by different rules altogether. Unlike many of my workers who merely eke out a living, his are filthy rich. Describing the good aspects of sex work, Aaron writes, "Often you will find yourself counting thousands of dollars at a time."[4]

Using his figures, I calculated that a competent sex worker can *gross* more than $175,000 per annum.[5] With such enormous sums at stake, the money will have to be laundered to be shielded from the prying eyes of the IRS. Well, at times, I too have dealt with my sex workers' laundry. The difference is that Aaron's workers may need to launder their money; mine use the washing machine and dryer in the garage to launder their clothes (saving time and quarters) while we have our session upstairs.

Throughout my books I have described how I (and other clients such as myself) can help sex workers with this or that little undertaking. Compared to the workers in Aaron's book, I am a pauper. They wouldn't need me (or my peers) to help them with anything.

But fortunately, it seems that there is hope for all clients. The upscale workers Aaron describes can also benefit by being buddies with their clients. "Another more legally questionable way in which you save significant amounts of money," he writes later in the same chapter, "is by having your clients vouch that the money they pay you are [sic] gifts, rather than income from your escorting services."[6] Rich clients help wealthy postmodern escorts launder their money; poorer clients help more humble sex workers wash their clothes.

While reading Aaron's book, I had a sudden flashback. When it came to merchandising, Lloyd, the protagonist of Chapter 7 of this book, was the most business-savvy sex worker I have ever met. For instance, every now and then, when things were slow, he would call me and say, "Haven't seen you for a while. I give discounts of twenty percent this week to early-bird customers." I am sure that had Lloyd discussed his offer at a sex workers' support group (there is one in San Francisco) in the new millennium, he would have been drummed out of the meeting!

Aaron's book brought the following incident to mind. I started seeing Lloyd in 1976, just after buying my house. All of my meetings with Lloyd were in calls. As I wrote in Chapter 7, Lloyd deliberately charged a lot of money for out calls because he preferred his customers to come to his place.

After becoming one of Lloyd's regulars, I suggested that he visit me sometime to see my new home and have our sex session there. "It has to be on a Saturday afternoon when I usually have no customers," he said.

"OK, Lloyd. How about Saturday next week?"

That Saturday, I showed Lloyd my home and served him cake and coffee. We chatted for a while, then had a leisurely sex session. When we were done, I paid him my usual twenty-five dollars, the preferred-customer in call fee. Twenty-four years later, after reading Aaron's new book, I realize that technically Lloyd was entitled to fifty dollars, his fee for an out call—maybe even one hundred dollars, or more; we were together for much longer than an hour. At the time, it seemed perfectly natural that Lloyd would visit me as a *friend*, and then we would have sex at his usual in call rate. This little vignette proves one point: No logical or ethical reason exists why a client cannot buy sex from a worker *and* simultaneously be his pal.

* * *

I close with seven guidelines that will help readers make their working relationships with escorts more friendly and emotionally intimate.

Respect

Sex workers deserve respect from clients. Clients, in turn, should expect the same from their workers.

Equality

Sex workers are neither worse nor better human beings than their clients. The fact that they have long dicks, muscular bodies, cute faces, or whatever, does not make them superior to clients who lack these attributes. Neither are they inferior to their clients because they are in the business of selling sex. Clients who have negative attitudes about paying for sex ought not to hire escorts in the first place.

Custom-Designed Relationships

Professionals (like architects and lawyers) are bound by a multitude of rules and regulations hamstringing their interactions with clients. Sex workers, on the other hand, are not bound by any external rules, regulations, or bylaws pertaining to how they can conduct their business. Workers and clients are free to make whatever arrangements they wish to fulfill *their* particular needs. This flexibility serves both parties equally well.

Create Win/Win Situations

Many years ago I made a date with a masseur. On the telephone, I stipulated a full-body massage as well as kissing. During the massage session, the masseur informed me that he really disliked kissing his clients. Naturally, I was angry that he wanted to renege on his promise, but I knew that if I held him to his agreement I would receive hateful kisses. "I'm not happy about you not keeping your promise, but I also don't want you to do something you detest," I told him. He didn't answer, continuing to massage in silence. Then, just before he "released" me, he gave me a long and affectionate French kiss. That evening, both of us came out winners.

Become a "Regular"

Regular clients usually get preferential treatment from their workers and are sometimes charged a lower fee. Regular "regulars" are good candidates for becoming virtual boyfriends. Michael and I recently reached a milestone—our 300th sex session. This could not have happened without a genuine liking for each other.

Make Appointments in Advance

In theory, clients can summon escorts in the wee hours of the morning after an evening of rejections at the bars. However, neither clients nor escorts are at their best so early in the day. Most likely, the session will be hurried and more costly. Advance appointments, made at a time convenient to both parties, are much more productive.

Prepare and Stick to a Budget

On vacations, I have sometimes indulged myself by hiring a sex worker on a daily basis. This kind of behavior can become addictive. An "escort budget" helps clients pace themselves to avoid going overboard.[7]

* * *

Recently, Michael and I celebrated our 300th sexual encounter. During my years with him, I have also conducted unremitting advertising campaigns on the Web and in gay publications seeking *steady* unpaid sex partners. In response, I have received dozens of e-mails and phone inquiries. Most of the respondents, even the ones who liked my photo or with whom I had a pleasant conversation on the phone, flaked out; we never met face to face. I suspect that for them the exercise of writing steamy e-mails or making risqué phone calls was excitement enough.

I did meet with a few respondents. Some had girlfriends and considered themselves straight; others were cheating on their gay lovers. Surprisingly, a number of them were Michael's age but better looking, more educated, and "hotter." Their lustfulness during our trysts led me to I believe that they enjoyed the encounter as much as I did. Nevertheless, from this group I saw only one man three times, the rest once or twice. Then they disappeared from my life. I do not know why they dropped me.

But I can explain why tonight Michael and I are starting the slow ascent toward our 400th encounter. The respondents to my ads played all sorts of unwholesome mind games with themselves and with me before, during, and after our encounters. In contrast, Michael and I play *in bed*. Before and after sex, no games at all come between us. This is because we have a crystal-clear understanding of what we want from these sessions. For Michael, it is his fee; for me, a good and *reliable* sex partner. Endeavoring to make each session as pleasant as possible for both parties is a matter of good business sense on Michael's part and plain common sense in my case. Because our experiences are always pleasant, we have come to like and appreciate each other genuinely.

Though some of the encounters with my free-access partners have been physically exhilarating, absolutely no emotional involvement has existed. We did not care about each other the least bit. But I care a great deal about Michael and my other regular sex workers. From my observations over many years, they feel the same way about me. We have become *virtual* boyfriends.

Appendix

Sex Workers' Web Sites

Below is a list of Web sites advertising the services of sex workers.* Sites of this kind come and go. By the time this book goes to print some of the entries may no longer be viable.

This list is merely a sample of what is available on the Web. Presenting this information is neither a recommendation nor an endorsement of any data contained in it.

www.escorts4you.com
www.MaleEscorts.com
www.Male4Malescorts.com
www.OzGay.com
http://Men-For-Rent.com
www.AmericanMale.net
www.M4MEscorts.com
www.EscortMale.com
www.Angloboyz.com
www.Adult-Entertainer.com
www.Gay-Male-Escorts-Worldwide.com
www.HiredKnights.com
www.pridesites.com
www.gayxsitement.com
www.meetlocalmen.com
www.gayescorts.org
http://books.dreambook.com/wellbelove/escorts.html
www.worldgay.com
www.Gay_Escort_Album.com
www.manpics.com
www.gaysexzone.com
www.trick-click.com
http://classyescort.1hwy.com
www.queerpersonals.com

*Courtesy of Bob Kane.

Notes

Preface

1. Joseph Itiel, *A Consumer's Guide to Male Hustlers* (Binghamton, NY: Harrington Park Press, 1998).

Prologue

1. Aaron Lawrence, *The Male Escort's Handbook: Your Guide to Getting Rich the Hard Way* (Warren, NJ: Late Night Press, 2000), pp. 184-185.

Chapter 1

1. Sex workers often take pride in pulling the wool over clients' eyes. See Aaron Lawrence, *Suburban Hustler: Stories of a Hi-Tech Callboy* (Warren, NJ: Late Night Press, 1999), p. 20.

2. By not deigning to give an "official" name to a vocation, the language says, in effect, that it ought not to exist. Biblical Hebrew offers an excellent example. The Old Testament abounds with female prostitutes (*zonah,* plural *zonot*). The famous Solomonic judgment (cutting the baby in half), for instance, was rendered in the case of two *zonot*—"harlots" (I Kings 3:16). Also recognized linguistically in the Old Testament are male and female cultic or temple prostitutes (*qadesh,* masc.; *qedeshah,* fem.). However much the authors of the Old Testament abhor cultic prostitution, they acknowledge the vocation. But when it comes to an ordinary male prostitute, they lack a proper noun and revert to cussing him out. "Thou shalt not bring the hire of a whore, or the price of a dog into the house of the LORD" (Deuteronomy 23:18 in the King James Version). The previous verse enjoins the Israelites from letting one of their sons become a *qadesh* or one of their daughters a *qedeshah.* In the next one, the noncultic, *zonah* male counterpart, is referred to as a "dog." The 1952 *Revised Standard Edition* (RSV) of the Bible inserts a footnote explaining the term dog: "Or a sodomite." The 1976 *Good News Bible: The Bible in Today's English Version* ignores the Hebrew distinction between *qedeshah* and *zonah* and refers to all of them, female as well as male, as "temple prostitutes." In this way the modern translators got rid of the Hebrew dog and the problem of coming up in English with a correct term for a male prostitute. The RSV's "sodomite" is certainly not an appropriate term. (The male prostitute of the Bible was much more likely to be the one who was sodomized.) For a full discussion of female prostitution in the Old Testament, see Jonathan Kirsch's *The Harlot by the Side of the Road: Forbidden Tales of the Bible* (New York: Ballantine Books, 1997), pp. 131-133.

3. Matt Adams, *Hustlers, Escorts, Porn Stars* (Las Vegas, NV: Matt Adams, 1998).

4. Charles Isherwood, *Wonder Bread and Ecstasy: The Life and Death of Joey Stefano* (Los Angeles, CA: Alyson Books, 1996), p. 84.

5. One of the first national gay publications, *The Advocate,* was founded "as a mimeographed sheet in Los Angeles in 1967" (*San Francisco Chronicle,* September 7, 2000, p. C6). For many years *The Advocate* ran nationwide listings of escorts. Some workers claimed that they got their best clients through ads in this publication.

6. This fitness craze is relatively new. When I arrived in San Francisco at the end of 1964 it was all about drag. The first outspoken gay organizations, such as the Society for Individual Rights, hashed and rehashed the same subject: Was it all right to raise funds through popular drag performances, even though it gave the wrong impression of the gay community?

7. The guys who work the streets in drag have a similar investment in their female attire. They serve mainly the "straight" market and I know relatively little about them. But when I wrote my gay guidebook to Costa Rica, I was admitted into a *cage aux folles,* interviewing a number of male prostitutes working the streets of San José in drag. Two of them told me that they engaged in prostitution so they would have enough money for their expensive drag outfits. See Joseph Itiel, Chapter 13, "An Interview with Ms. Universe," *Pura Vida: A Travel Guide to Gay and Lesbian Costa Rica* (San Francisco: Orchid House, 1993), pp. 96-97.

8. John Preston, *Hustling: A Gentleman's Guide to the Fine Art of Homosexual Prostitution* (New York: Masquerade Books, 1994).

9. Adams, *Hustlers, Escorts, Porn Stars,* p. 95

Chapter 3

1. Aaron Lawrence, who claims to be the highest-paid escort in New York City and environs, recounts how much he liked to service everyone, uglies included, *before* he became a sex worker. Aaron Lawrence, *Suburban Hustler: Stories of a Hi-Tech Callboy* (Warren, NJ: Late Night Press, 1999), pp. 10-18. Aaron Lawrence's second book, *The Male Escort's Handbook: Your Guide to Getting Rich the Hard Way* (Warren, NJ: Late Night Press, 2000) gives a balanced view of the joys and sorrows of working as an escort and, most important, the potential for striking it rich.

2. *The Male Escorts of San Francisco,* video produced by M. Link, 1992.

3. Rick Whitaker, *Assuming the Position: A Memoir of Hustling* (New York: Four Walls Eight Windows, 1992).

4. Ibid., p. 153

5. Ibid., p. 126.

6. Matt Bernstein Sycamore, *Tricks and Treats: Sex Workers Write About Their Clients* (Binghamton, NY: Harrington Park Press, 2000).

7. Two sex workers told me of clients shooting up in front of them and used needles scattered all over the place. The fear of accidentally sticking themselves was very real.

8. Joseph Itiel, *Philippine Diary: A Gay Guide to the Philippines* (San Francisco: International Wavelength, 1989). See Chapter 2, "Straight is Gay and Gay is Gayer."

9. Lawrence, *Suburban Hustler,* p. 11.

Chapter 4

1. *The Male for Male Escort Review,* "Escort Etiquette," adapted by Australian escort Mark. Online at: <http:/www.male4maleescorts.com/features/Escortpercent20 Etiquette.htm>. Accessed September 4, 2000.
2. Michael's problems with phone calls are compounded by his full-time job. According to him, it serves no purpose to return calls received earlier in the day when he gets off work. As a result, most calls go unanswered.
3. See Joseph Itiel, "Dirty Young Men." *Chiron Rising,* #66, 1995.

Chapter 5

1. This subject is taken up in various parts of Itiel's *A Consumer's Guide to Male Hustlers.* See index entries under "Massage."

Chapter 6

1. Sam Steward, *Understanding the Male Hustler* (Binghamton, NY: Harrington Park Press, 1996). See introduction by Dr. John De Cecco, p. xii.
2. Sex workers often "retire" from escorting only to reemerge again a month, a year, or even a decade later.
3. *Macbeth,* Act I, Scene III.
4. While some sex workers claim that their work ruins their sexuality, others have lovers who are in the same line of business. A few even have supportive nonsex worker lovers who allow them to escort and maintain the relationship. One sex worker dedicated his hustling memoir to his lover. See Aaron Lawrence, *Suburban Hustler: Stories of a Hi-Tech Callboy* (Warren, NJ: Late Night Press, 1998).

Chapter 7

1. Arguably, the street hustling scene in New York City was (is?) even harsher than in San Francisco. See Robert P. McNamara, *The Times Square Hustler: Male Prostitution in New York City* (Westport, CT: Praeger Publishers, 1994).
2. Due to pagers, today's arrangements are somewhat *less* safe. See *A Consumer's Guide,* p. 165, footnote 8.
3. See index in *A Consumer's Guide* for entries under "Alfonso."

Chapter 8

1. This type of request can become dangerous to the sex worker. After the session is over some clients will refuse to pay the worker because the worker enjoyed it as much as the client did. The client will justify his refusal to pay by telling the worker, "I gave you what *you* asked for."
2. At the end of the 1970s, *before* AIDS was a known disease, some alarm bells went off. The late David B. Goodstein, owner of *The Advocate* at the time, even commissioned a book on this subject, *The Advocate Guide to Gay Health,* by R.D. Fenwick (New York: E.P. Dutton, 1978). It features a chapter titled "The Hazards of Sex" in addition to specific information on sexually transmitted diseases.

Chapter 11

1. Chubbies are not universally disdained. They do have their admirers and have a small representation in the sex workers' community. Rafael, in *The Male Escorts of San Francisco* (video produced by M. Link, 1992), describes himself as a "Call Bear, 5' 11", 230 lbs., balding, an old guy." Because of his age and weight he has fewer clients who prefer his physical type.

2. See "Self-Image Enhancement" in Itiel, *A Consumer's Guide to Male Hustlers,* p. 34.

Chapter 12

1. One of the first national gay publications, *The Advocate,* was founded "as a mimeographed sheet in Los Angeles in 1967" (*San Francisco Chronicle,* September 7, 2000, p. C6). For many years it featured a comprehensive escort list.

2. Rick Whitaker, *Assuming the Position: A Memoir of Hustling* (New York: Four Walls Eight Windows, 1992).

3. Don Shewey, "Sex Work As Health Care: Confessions of a 'Pleasure Activist,'" *genre,* March 2000, pp. 54-59.

4. *Bay Area Reporter,* September 7, 2000, p. 48.

Chapter 13

1. Aaron Lawrence, *The Male Escort's Handbook: Your Guide to Getting Rich the Hard Way* (Warren, NJ: Late Night Press, 2000).

2. Ibid., p. 188.

3. Curiously, even at $350 an hour—Aaron's fee—tips for sex workers are still under discussion. My understanding is that business owners are never tipped. It is the *underpaid* employees who deserve them.

4. Lawrence, *The Male Escort's Handbook,* p. 205.

5. Two daily sessions at $350, five days a week, multiplied by fifty weeks (allowing for a two-week vacation), comes out to $175,000. But since many sessions last longer than one hour, and overnight calls command a much higher rate, we are really looking at closer to $200,000.

6. Lawrence, *The Male Escort's Handbook,* p. 213.

7. Aaron has restricted a client's number of monthly sessions so the latter would not face financial ruin. See Lawrence, *The Male Escort's Handbook,* p. 128.

Index

A Consumer's Guide ..., ix
  and agencies, 21
  and escorting, 15
  and fake orgasm, 7
  and Gabriel (story of), 11
  and hip-hop dancing, 159
  and massage, 55
  and Michael (story of), 42
  and Misha (story of), 122-123
  and overcharging, 12, 41
  and preferred client discount, 46
  and psyching oneself into hustler
    role, 1
  and regular appointments, 25
  and rejection, 125
  and sex acts, agreeing on, 75
  and sex worker as lover, 55
  and sleep, avoiding, 130
  and street hustlers, 66
  and tipping, 22
Adams, Matt, 15, 18
Ads, personal, 13, 25, 66, 86, 118, 124
advance booking, 25-29, 135
age, lying about, 117
agencies, 21-24, 104
Alex (Lloyd), story of, 66-72, 133
Alfonso, story of, 7
anorexia, 109
answering machine, 69
"apprentice," 23
arousal, 2
artificial rush, 21
ass to ass massage, 52-53
*Assuming the Position: A Memoir of
    Hustling,* 31-32, 35, 59
attitude, 31-33
  of mature sex worker, 122

bathhouse, 33, 37-40
  Barcelona, 125-128, 129-131
Bay Area Reporter, 14, 44

Beauregard, story of, 63, 73-84
billable hours, 42
Billy, story of, 89-95
bottom, 2, 123-124
boundaries, 42, 43
budget, sticking to, 135

"call boy," 12, 15
chubbies, 109
circumcised sex worker, 51, 99, 119
client
  friendship with, 80
  guidelines for, 134-135
  and sex-plus relationships, 55-63
  socializing with, 44
  stories
    James, 3-9
    Roland, 3
  as sugar daddy, 102-108
  as type-oriented, 16
  versus john or trick, 18
climax. *See* orgasm
code of ethics, sex worker, 132
condom, 5, 6, 7, 120
Consumer Price Index, 102
custom-designed relationships, 134

danger, 35
dating versus escorting, 37
De Cecco, John, 55
"dirty young men," free sex with, 46
discount, preferred client, 46, 128
"Dreamy erotic Creole," masseur, 85
"drop," agency's cut, 22
drugs, 103

economic hardship, hustling due to, 35-36
Edmond, story of, 118-121

Elgin, Jerry, 33-34
elimination of agency, 23
elite escorts, 15
equality, 134
erection, lost, 7
escort, 65-66, 101. *See also* sex worker
    guidelines for working with, 134-135
escort budget, 135
"escort etiquette," 42
"Escorts and Models," ad, 15
Étienne, story of, 48
external prejudice, 32
eyes, closing of, 7

Filipino gays, 37
fitness craze, 17
foot massage, 49
foreplay, 4
"foretalk," 5
full-body massage, 47

Gabriel, story of, 11-12
gay publications, sex worker
        advertisements in, 17, 25, 117
gonorrhea, 82
"gym rat," 17

handyman, sex worker as, 93
hard sex, 48
health check, lack of, 22
Helmut, story of, 126-132
hip-hop dancing, 59
HIV negative, 99
HIV positive, 11
"honorarium," 113
housekeeper, sex worker as, 77-78
hustler. *See also* sex worker
    alternate terms for, 12
    hustling clients, 13-14
    as independent contractor, *x*, 50
    as a professional, 17, 41-46
    and socializing with clients, 44
Hustlers, Escorts, Porn Stars, 15
*Hustling: A Gentleman's Guide to the
        Fine Art of Homosexual
        Prostitution,* 17-18
"hustling survivor," 80

in call, escort, 66, 67
income, sex worker, 132
independent contractor, hustler as, *x*, 50
inexperience, sex and, 110, 111
Internet, 2, 3
    advertising on, 24-25, 137
intimacy, nonsexual, 12
Isherwood, Charles, 16

James, story of, 3-9
José Luis, story of, 36

Katz, Marvin, 102-108
kiss
    aggressive, 6, 70
    inexperience with, 110, 111
    intimate, 4, 120
    in public, 27
    refusal to, 128
    women only, 99

Latin American hustlers, 36
Lawrence, Aaron, 31, 131-133
liar, hustler as, 13-14, 117
Lloyd (Alex), story of, 66-72, 133
lover, sex worker as, 55-63
lubricant, condom, 5, 6-7, 120

The Male Escort's Handbook, 131
The Male Escorts of San Francisco
    (video), 31
"Male to Male Personals," Internet site,
    2-3
"Man Seeking Man" section, 109
massage, 47-54
massage table, 47
masseur
    author's search for, 85-95
    stories of
        Edmond, 118-121
        Sundaram, 49-54
        Van, 86-89
mature sex worker, 117, 118-124
mentor, author as, 97-108

Michael, story of, 42-46, 57-58, 135-136
Misha, story of, 122-123
model, 15, 78-79
"Models and Escorts," 73
"most favorite client" rate, 26

Native American partner, 118-121
nipples, biting, 70
nonsexual intimacy, 12

observe boundaries, 42, 43
"Older Seeks Younger" ad, 109
Omar, story of, 23, 56-57, 97-108
oral sex, 6, 56
    inexperience with, 110
orgasm, 8, 28
    fake, 7
    sex games and, 70
    simultaneous, 120
Oscar, story of, 26-28, 29, 61-63
Our Lady of Medjugorje, 83-84
overcharging, 12, 41
overweight, sex worker, 109-115, 119

pager, 17, 87
Patrick, story of, 58-59
penetration, 8, 48
    refusal, 91
    sex worker enjoyment in, 75, 100
person with AIDS (PWA), 27
personal ads, 13, 25, 66, 86, 118, 124
phone calls, screening, 23
photographs, 62
    exchanging, 3
    on Web, 25
poor performance, hustler, 13
porn star, as elite escort, 15, 16
position of masseur, 51-52
Preston, John, 17-18
pretty, man as, 79
Prisoner of War, sex game, 69-70
professional, hustler as, 17, 41-46
prostitute, definition of, 14-15

regular client, becoming a, 134-135
rejection, 125
relationships, sex-plus, 56-63
release massage, 47, 48, 87, 88, 118
"rent boy," 12, 16
reservation, making a, 22
respect, 134
Roland, story of, 3
Ron, story of, 13-14

safe(r) sex instructions, 7
security check, lack of, 22
self-image enhancement, 113
self-loathing, 31-32
sex acts, agreement on, 75
sex games, 78, 79
    Prisoner of War, 69-70
    water sports, 105-106
sex room, "trickery," 51, 53
"Sex Work As Health care," 123
sex worker. *See also* escort; hustler
    advertisements in gay publications, 17, 25
    advertisements on the Web, 24-25, 137
    author experiment as, 1-9
    code of ethics, 132
    gay bias toward, 33-34
    as handyman, 93
    as housekeeper, 77-78
    income, 132
    inexperienced, 110, 111
    mature, 118-124
    overweight, 109-115, 119
    pleasing a, 75
    socializing with, 44, 77, 94-95
    special relationships with clients, 56-63
    stories of
        Alex (Lloyd), 66-72, 133
        Alfonso, 7
        Beauregard, 63, 73-84
        Billy, 89-95
        Étienne, 48
        Gabriel, 11-12
        Helmut, 126-132
        José Luis, 36
        Lloyd (Alex), 66-72, 133
        Michael, 42-46, 57-58, 135-136

sex worker, stories of *(continued)*
    Misha, 122-123
    Omar, 23, 56-57, 97-108
    Oscar, 26-28, 29, 61-63
    Patrick, 58-59
    Ron, 13-14
    Terry, 59-61
    Winston Lee, 43, 109-115
sexual magnetism, 99
sexually transmitted diseases, 82-83
Shewey, Don, 123
sleep, avoiding, 130
socializing, 44, 77, 94-95
soft sex, 48
spontaneity, 25-29
Stefano, Joey, 16
street, picked up on, 27-28, 62
street hustler, 16
"sugar daddyism," *x*, 102-108
sugar son, 102-108
Sundaram, story of, 49-54
supplemental security income (SSI), 11
Sycamore, Matt Bernstein, 32-33

tantra massage, 52-53
Terry, story of, 59-61
threats, 62
time management, poor, 113
tipping, 22-23
top, 2, 3
"trickery," sex room, 51, 53
Tricks and Treats, 32-33
type-oriented clients, 16

Van, story of, 86-89
Viagra, 2, 5
virtual boyfriend, *ix,* 43, 136

water sports, 105-106
Whitaker, Rick, 31-32, 33, 35, 59, 122
"wildness," 8, 9
Winston Lee, story of, 43, 109-115
win/win situations, creating, 134
World Wide Web, advertising on,
    24-25, 137

Order a copy of this book with this form or online at:
http://www.haworthpressinc.com/store/product.asp?sku=4558

SEX WORKERS AS VIRTUAL BOYFRIENDS

_____in hardbound at $29.95 (ISBN: 1-56023-190-4)

_____in softbound at $14.95 (ISBN: 1-56023-191-2)

COST OF BOOKS_____

OUTSIDE USA/CANADA/
MEXICO: ADD 20%____

POSTAGE & HANDLING_____
(US: $4.00 for first book & $1.50
for each additional book)
Outside US: $5.00 for first book
& $2.00 for each additional book)

SUBTOTAL_____

in Canada: add 7% GST____

STATE TAX____
(NY, OH & MIN residents, please
add appropriate local sales tax)

FINAL TOTAL____
(If paying in Canadian funds,
convert using the current
exchange rate, UNESCO
coupons welcome.)

❑　**BILL ME LATER:** ($5 service charge will be added)
(Bill-me option is good on US/Canada/Mexico orders only;
not good to jobbers, wholesalers, or subscription agencies.)

❑　Check here if billing address is different from
shipping address and attach purchase order and
billing address information.

Signature_____

❑　**PAYMENT ENCLOSED: $_____**

❑　**PLEASE CHARGE TO MY CREDIT CARD.**

❑ Visa　❑ MasterCard　❑ AmEx　❑ Discover
❑ Diner's Club　❑ Eurocard　❑ JCB

Account # _____

Exp. Date_____

Signature_____

Prices in US dollars and subject to change without notice.

NAME_____
INSTITUTION_____
ADDRESS_____
CITY_____
STATE/ZIP_____
COUNTRY_____ COUNTY (NY residents only)_____
TEL_____ FAX_____
E-MAIL_____

May we use your e-mail address for confirmations and other types of information? ❑ Yes ❑ No
We appreciate receiving your e-mail address and fax number. Haworth would like to e-mail or fax special
discount offers to you, as a preferred customer. **We will never share, rent, or exchange your e-mail address
or fax number.** We regard such actions as an invasion of your privacy.

Order From Your Local Bookstore or Directly From
The Haworth Press, Inc.
10 Alice Street, Binghamton, New York 13904-1580 • USA
TELEPHONE: 1-800-HAWORTH (1-800-429-6784) / Outside US/Canada: (607) 722-5857
FAX: 1-800-895-0582 / Outside US/Canada: (607) 722-6362
E-mail: getinfo@haworthpressinc.com
PLEASE PHOTOCOPY THIS FORM FOR YOUR PERSONAL USE.
www.HaworthPress.com

BOF02